Physical Characteristics of the
Caucasian Mountain Dog

(from the Fédération Cynologique Internationale breed standard)

Back: Very wide, straight, muscular.

Tail: Set high.

Coat: The fur is natural, coarse with strongly developed lighter undercoat.

Color: Various grays. Mostly light to rust-colored tones. Also rust-colored, straw, yellow, white, earth-colored, striped, but also spotted and piebald.

Hind Limbs: Seen from the side, knee joint somewhat stretched out. Short lower leg. Powerful ankle joints which are wide and somewhat stretched. A vertical line should run from the buttocks towards the middle of the ankle joints and the metacarpus.

Abdomen: Moderate tuck-up.

Paws: Large oval form, domed and well closed.

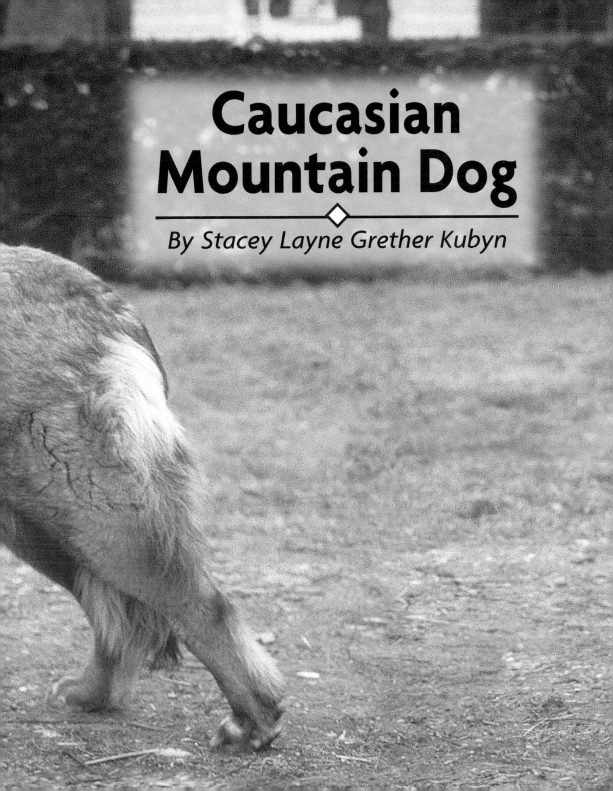

Caucasian Mountain Dog

By Stacey Layne Grether Kubyn

Contents

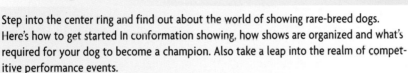

KENNEL CLUB BOOKS: **CAUCASIAN MOUNTAIN DOG**
ISBN: 1-59378-345-0

Copyright © 2005 Kennel Club Books, LLC
308 Main St., Allenhurst, New Jersey USA 07711
Cover Design Patented: US 6,435,559 B2 • Printed in South Korea

Photography by Isabelle Francais
with additional photographs by

Bernd Brinkmann, Paulette Braun, T.J. Calhoun, Alan and Sandy Carey, Carolina Biological Supply, Juliette Cunliffe, David Dalton, Fleabusters Rx for Fleas, Carol Ann Johnson, Bill Jonas, Stacey Kubyn, Dr. Dennis Kunkel, Tam C. Nguyen, Phototake, Jean Claude Revy and Alice van Kempen.

Illustrations by Patricia Peters.

The Caucasian Mountain Dog has been at man's service for more than 2,000 years. The breed was trained to protect both sheep and shepherds in cold mountainous conditions.

HISTORY OF THE

CAUCASIAN MOUNTAIN DOG

"Second century AD stone carvings of tall, powerful dogs...Tales of great shaggy beasts saving their owners from various dangers...The heroic dog, 'Topush,' killing over a hundred wolves while protecting the family flock...Aralez, old Armenian beneficent dog-like spirits, licking the wounds of those who fell in battle, thus healing or resurrecting them..."

INTRODUCTION

In times and places of danger, when the conditions of life are harsh, the partnership between dog and man is forged by a special urgency. For here the dog must be large, powerful and unflinchingly brave. The dog must be devoted and incorruptible not by training but rather innately, or by the necessity of a hard existence.

The Caucasian Mountain Dog is such a dog: a wall of determination bounding forward, always placing himself before the threat, charging forward with a fury and determination that harken back to a primitive epoch, when the dog might any day or any night be called upon to fight to his death in the service of his partnership with man. The Caucasian Mountain Dog is a dog with over 2,000-year-old roots in the remote mountainous region of the Caucasus in southeastern Europe, the legendary land of towering mountains, winding valleys and endless steppes, where one can envision Greek mythology leaping to life: Prometheus, demigod of the Titans, chained by Zeus as punishment for giving fire and the arts to mankind, and Jason, leader of the Argonauts, in search of the Golden Fleece.

IN HIS NATIVE LANGUAGE. . .
The Caucasian Mountain Dog breed is called "Nagazi" in the Georgian Republic, one of his countries of origin.

OUR BREED IN THE 21ST CENTURY

The Caucasian Mountain Dog is known by many names around the world. Though the Russian name for the breed "Kavkazskaya Ovcharka", translates most directly into "Caucasian Shepherd Dog," we decided to call this book (and breed) Caucasian Mountain Dog to adhere to the popular US name for the breed *and its* AKC-chosen name. Just as the breed is known by different names, type varies around the world, too. The Caucasian is a breed in transition from native landrace to breeding in accordance with the modern breed standard. The photographs in this book reflect the wide variety of type in today's Caucasian population around the world, including the author's own breeding, the heavier Russian-bred dogs, as well as many European-bred dogs, show dogs and pet dogs.

The Caucasian Mountain Dog is a dog of legends from a time when age-old stories were passed down around the campfires among the inhabitants of remote villages. And so they would sit, our European forefathers, and tell the stories of the great bear-like dog that would strike down an enemy, sacrificing himself to protect the flock and family. During the 20th century, the Caucasian Mountain Dog was removed from his remote Caucasus homeland to Asia. In the former USSR, the breed was utilized for guarding factories and military establishments. Today this noble ancient breed links the past to the present and has captured the hearts of dog fanciers throughout the world.

As I write these lines from the comfortable study of my home in Ohio, two of my Caucasian Mountain Dogs lie here by my side, still on guard, still my partners. I see their watchful readiness and feel the confidence and security they bring to my home—the same qualities that the shepherds of the high Caucasus villages admired two millennia ago. The Caucasian Mountain Dogs have not changed so very much in all of that time, but the world of men surely has. Although the days of passing legends are far behind in our modern world, perhaps these pages will at least be a small window to this piece of canine history.

MEET THE CAUCASIAN MOUNTAIN DOG

The Caucasian Mountain Dog is a breed belonging to the ancient molosser group of primitive flock-guardian or livestock-guardian dogs and is closely related to the flock guardians of Tibet, other parts of Asia and the European mountains. This flock-guardian subdivision includes the Tibetan Mastiff, Spanish Mastiff, Anatolian Karabash, Great Pyrenees, Estrela Mountain Dog and Kuvasz. The Caucasian's age-old duty, like that of his flock-guardian brethren, is to defend sheep and village from four- and two-legged predators—wolves, big cats, bears and human thieves.

The Caucasian Mountain Dog is indigenous to the Caucasus region, an isolated mountainous finger of land extending 750 miles from the Black Sea to the Caspian Sea. The main range, the Greater Caucasus, is a majestic chain of snow-capped peaks. Several passes divide the North Caucasus, which slopes down to the Kuban steppe, a major grain region, from Transcaucasia. The Lesser Caucasus is an extension of the Iranian plateau with pastures and forests in the uplands and orchards and vineyards in the valleys.

The breed hails from the following countries: the Georgian Republic, Armenia, Azerbaijan, Dagestan and surrounding areas. While Russia is considered the modern motherland of the Caucasian breed, the many peoples of the Caucasus have held a working partnership with the breed for thousands of years and are diverse in culture and language, different from Russian, and not of Slavic origin. To these people, the dogs are known as "Nagazi" or "Shepherd Dog" (in the Georgian Republic) and "Gampr" (in Armenia). The peoples of the Caucasus also refer to their dogs according to the work they perform, their appearance or their characteristics. Thus one may hear the dogs referred to as "Mgeli Dzaghli" (wolf-dogs) in

OVCHARKA BREEDS
The Caucasian Mountain Dog, known as the Kavkazskaya Ovcharka in Russia, is one of the native flock-guardian dogs known as "ovcharkas." The word "ovcharka" is a Slavic-based word, meaning "shepherd dog" or "sheepdog." Among the breed's ovcharka cousins are the Central Asian Ovcharka and South Russian Ovcharka, the former of which is leggier and less coated than the Caucasian and the latter of which is densely coated and usually colored in solid white.

Central Asian Ovcharka.

the Georgian Republic or "Kurt Kopek" (wolf-dogs) in Azerbaijan, while black-masked dogs are called "Topush" in Armenia.

Only more recently has the breed become known as an "Ovcharka," the Slavic-based Russian-language word that translates roughly into "shepherd dog" or

COLOR RANGE

The Caucasian Mountain Dog is one of the few flock-guardian breeds that is typically agouti gray or fawn in color. Only 3% of the breed is all white.

"sheepdog." In Russia, the country of origin as designated by cynological organizations, the breed is referred to as the Kavkazskaya Ovcharka, which translates most closely as "Caucasian Shepherd Dog." But because the breed is a mountain-type guardian of the flock and not a herding dog, many modern fanciers refer to the breed as the "Caucasian Mountain Dog," as we do here.

EARLY ORIGINS

Lack of written records leaves questions regarding exactly how and when the flock-guardian dogs of the Caucasus originated. Several theories are proposed, but none can be proven, and it is possible that flock-guardian dogs entered the Caucasus through several routes. One romantic theory suggests that the Caucasian Mountain Dog is a completely independent and unique breed, originating in the Caucasus as a domestication of local wolves by the settlers of the region. The theory more often promulgated is that the Caucasian, as with the other molosser-type dogs, is a direct natural descendant of the Tibetan Mastiff, which entered the region through trade routes.

Other writers speculate that the Caucasian Mountain Dog was created by purposeful crossing of mastiff-type dogs with sheep-herding spitz-like dogs to produce a hardy breed, resistant to the cold, with sufficient size and fierceness. Yet another theory suggests that the breed developed from pariah dogs of Mesopotamia, which accompanied the nomadic people during their trek across the Asian continent. Over the centuries, parts of the Caucasus and surrounding regions were invaded and conquered by different cultures that may have brought their own dogs with them.

We do know that DNA evidence proves the wolf to be the ancestor of today's domestic dog. Skeletal remains of a strain of wolf, *Canis volgensis,* were discovered along the river Volga, Transcausasia, Yakutsk region, and in northern China. A commonly held theory is that 14,000 to 16,000 years ago, a mutually beneficial, cooperative effort began between individuals of a wolf population and man, signifying the beginning of the domesticated dog. The first agricultural pursuits and the domestication of sheep and goats also coincide with this timetable. The dog's first job for man may well have been guarding livestock from his hungry wolf ancestors.

Dog skeletal remains dating to 4000 BC, depicting dogs with massive skulls and a gradual transition from muzzle to strong jaws, were discovered near the Russian

The breed, here called the Caucasian Sheep Dog, was featured on a postage stamp of the Georgian Republic in 1996.

town of Bologoj and the Ladoga Water Canal. The Bronze Age dog, *Canis familiaris matris optimae,* or, as translated from the Latin, "dog of the best mother," was large, with a wedge-like skull and a long muzzle. It is thought to have been common in the steppes around the Black Sea and northern Caucasus by 2000 BC.

Iberian tribes were spread from the East to the West more than 4,000 years ago, settling the Caucasus (then called eastern Iberia) in fortified villages. Their survival depended on the safekeeping of their goats, sheep and cows, which grazed seasonal pastures and required protection from the fierce predators of the region. These settlers maintained trade relations with Asia and the

CROPPING TRADITIONS

Herdsmen crop a puppy's ears horizontally and bluntly close to the head to prevent their loss to the teeth of a predatory wolf. Legend says that the mother dog must consume the ear flaps, for if they are eaten by a wolf, the puppy will never have the strength to defend against him. Ear cropping continues throughout Russia and the former Soviet Union but is outlawed in some other parts of Europe. Most breeders in the US crop their dogs' ears.

ian manuscript of antiquity predating the second century AD references the shepherd dogs of the area. In the Azerbaijan mountain area, pictures are carved in stone of dogs drawn very tall and powerful. Folk tales and legends often make mention of large shaggy dogs who saved their owners from various dangers.

We know that western Iberia was conquered by the Celts, who were thought to have brought with them dogs called "hunting mastiffs." The crossing of the so-called Iberian Sheepdogs and Celtic dogs is speculated by some to have produced the Pyrenean Mastiff and Spanish Mastiff, while the Caucasian branch of the flock-guardian dog family remained isolated and consistent in type, explaining the unique appearance of the Caucasian Mountain Dog today.

THE CAUCASIAN MOUNTAIN DOG IN RUSSIA

The Caucasian Mountain Dog is said to have been known in Russia since the Caucasian wars of 1765–1774 and possibly earlier in the Transcaucasus, native grasslands inhabited by early Russians.

The Spanish Mastiff (TOP) and the Pyrenean Mastiff (BOTTOM) share many similarities with the Caucasian Mountain Dog in looks, background and ability.

Mediterranean. With the advent of slave trading came the additional need for personal and family protection. Ancient Greek and Roman writers made reference to the flock-guardian dogs of the Caucasus. Aristotle and Terenius are said to have called such dogs "Iberian Sheepdogs." An Armen-

> ### HOW RARE IS RARE?
> While still considered a rare breed throughout Europe and the Americas, the Russian National stud book records over 41,000 Caucasian Mountain Dogs.

But the beginning of the modern history of the Caucasian breed in Russia is reported to be the 1920s, when the breed was sought as a livestock guardian dog to defend cattle and sheep from Russian wolf packs, jackals and bears. In some areas, organized dog-fighting matches provided entertainment and a selection criterion for the best four-footed warriors. The extraordinary territorial-guarding and predator dispatching abilities of the breed were highly acclaimed, and, by the 1930s, the Caucasian breed was a legend throughout Russia.

One such Russian legend tells of a severe and sudden snowstorm in which 400 head of sheep were separated from the rest of the flock and lost. Three Caucasian Mountain Dogs who were guarding the sheep also vanished. Long searches were conducted but proved fruitless. Six weeks later, some herdsmen discovered the lost flock grazing on a pasture, guarded by three emaciated Caucasian Mountain Dogs. Both the adult sheep and newly born lambs, numbering now about 500 head, were saved by the dogs that never left their charges. The dogs apparently survived on rodents hunted down for food and bore the scars of countless encounters with wolves and other predators.

During this same period, the Soviet Red Army and NKVD (later known as KGB) kennels

EVER-WATCHFUL GUARDIAN
Of course, the Caucasian Mountain Dog was bred to guard his flock from intruders, both lupine and human. There is a common saying about the breed that the Caucasian is so watchful that he sleeps with one eye open.

took hundreds of Caucasian dogs from the rural areas for use in the guarding of factories, storage sites, military installations and prisons. Over the next half-century, special Soviet-State-run kennels bred "chain-dogs," with some kennels selecting for dogs with large and heavy-set bodies, guarding instinct and extreme ferocity instead of the historical athletic, well-balanced flock- and family-protection dogs of the Caucasus.

Some of the army kennels are reputed to have extensively crossed the Caucasian Mountain Dog with other breeds in an attempt to make the Caucasian dogs larger and also to try to create new breeds. Russian authors Alexander Inshakov and Eugene Tsigelnitsky write, "The practice of crossings became very common during the breeding of Moscow's Watchdog (Caucasian Sheepdog x St. Bernard) and the Moscow Diver (Caucasian Sheepdog x Newfoundland)." Nobody knows how many cross-bred dogs had been registered as Caucasian Sheepdogs during that period. Such a way of breeding and selection produced the *enfant terrible* of the army kennels: extremely rough, huge and heavy with too-

heavy heads and poor hips and movements (movement not being important for chain-dogs). Such Caucasians often had bad temperaments: they attacked everything around, becoming dangerous even for the handlers. This type is widely spread over the country, but it is undesirable from the point of view of private owners or organized breeders.

Organized breeders throughout Russia have indeed worked to preserve the pure Caucasian Mountain Dog. The first post-war dog show reports in Moscow date to 1947. By the 1960s, the breed was flourishing in Moscow, with 179 Caucasian Mountain Dogs exhibited in 1964 at the 28th Moscow City Show. The first registered Caucasian Mountain Dog in what was then called Leningrad appeared in the 1960s in the stud book of the Working Dog Club and in the show catalog during this time. The best and most famous Caucasian dog populations became concentrated in the big cities: Moscow, Leningrad, Ivanovo, Nizhni, Novgorod and Perm.

These dogs were also kept in kennels and used for guarding factories and storehouses and were shown at the Agricultural Fair of the USSR as an achievement of the Soviet national farmer. Selection was geared toward property protection, with emphasis placed on stable temperament. All working dogs had to be rated at a show with marks of "Excellent" or "Very Good" in order to be bred, and had to pass obedience and protection tests in order to then be judged on physical conformation at a show. One such temperament/training test was the "KS," which included a minimal obedience requirement along with a high defense reaction. The dog had to exhibit aggressiveness toward strangers who attempted to pass the dog's tie-out when the dog's owner left the dog tied with a command to "Watch." Show dogs during this time were quite ferocious and often came into the show ring wearing muzzles.

The advent of electronic intruder-alert systems and the hardships accompanying the breakup of the Soviet Union in the early 1990s resulted in a decline in the number of guard dogs employed in Russian factories. Dogs need to be fed, and their necessity declined as electronic security systems were installed. To add infection to injury, an epidemic of infectious hepatitis in Moscow spread throughout the breed at this time. Breeders abandoned their kennel programs and closed up. Part of the best Caucasian Mountain Dog populations in the big city kennels were lost.

Simultaneously the breed came into fashion with the Russian general public. Clubs fragmented

GOOD AND BAD LUCK

There is a superstition in some parts of the Caucasus that forbids photographing Caucasian Mountain Dogs for fear that the dogs will be cursed by an "evil eye" and become sick and die. Another legend says that clothing spun from the undercoat of the Caucasian will impart good health upon the wearer.

and the breed suffered a very difficult period of transition. Female dogs of any origin were bred to the same males. The lines and families were broken down and became difficult to trace, and numerous pedigrees were falsified. About the Kavkazskaya Ovcharka, *Russia Magazine* in 1998 reported that "Dozens of organizations all over the country were breeding dogs and giving out the hastily made pedigrees. Any contacts between

A theory proposes that the Caucasian breed and other Molosser flock-guardian breeds descended from the Tibetan Mastiff, shown here.

1995, the Fédération Cynologique Internationale (FCI) recognized the Russian Kynological Federation (RKF) and named Russia as the parent country of the Caucasian Mountain Dog. The RKF's new program, known as the Russian National Breed Clubs, united each breed's parent clubs, resulting in one club representing each breed. Further, the Russian National Club was formed to unite the various regional clubs. The RKF maintains a stud book for the Caucasian Mountain Dog and issues pedigrees with holograms and dog tattoo numbers. Some Caucasians registered in the Russian National Stud Book have 17-generation pedigrees.

the specialists were impossible, as they were afraid of revealing their shady business. Some of them didn't trust anybody and withdrew into themselves; others were indifferent to anything and cared only of their own males mating. The breed broke like a mirror, and the smaller the fragments were, the more distorted and abnormal the reflection was. Today the ties are gradually settling, the number of those who want to make a profit out of the breeding decreases, and only the true enthusiasts stay. Time will show which of them is right."

Despite technology, hepatitis and puppy booms, dedicated breeders throughout the former USSR persevered through the darkest of breed times. Today strong breed clubs exist in Russia, furthering the breed as a property guardian and family protector. In

THE BREED OUTSIDE RUSSIA
By the turn of the 20th century, the Caucasian Mountain Dog found its way outside Russia. Through the efforts of Gustav Radde, German researcher and founder of the Caucasian Museum, the Swiss cynologists Prof. Heim and Conrad Keller were made aware of the breed. Canine literature and encyclopedias published during the early and mid-1900s also provide brief descriptions.

The first exhibited Caucasian Mountain Dogs outside Russia were shown in 1930 at the German National Exhibition in Nuremberg. Likely these dogs were sold to German breeders by Russian sources, though their actual origins and history in Germany remain unclear. According to some writers, World War II halted breeding efforts, which were resumed after the war by the military, the police, state sheep-breeding farms and a few private breeders. Other sources identify 1969 as the year that the breed was established in East Germany and 1979 as the year that the breed became established in West Germany. By 1987 the breed had spread to Finland. Considered a "National Treasure," export from the USSR was still forbidden as late as 1989, but individuals of the breed continued to cross into other European countries and the West. In 1990, the Caucasian Mountain Dog breed was introduced in the United States, and the US parent club was organized by author Stacey Kubyn of Esquire Caucasians (www.esquirecaucasians.com).

Today increasing numbers of the modern standardized Caucasian Mountain Dog of Russia can be found in many countries around the globe. The Fédération Cynologique Internationale recognizes the breed and holds shows in Europe and South America. Likewise, alternative clubs also exist and are growing in popularity. In 1995, the breed was recognized in the United States by the United Kennel Club, now listed as the Caucasian Ovcharka. The breed is eligible for the American Kennel Club's FSS (Foundation Stock Service, a record-keeping service for breeds not currently AKC-registered) as the Caucasian Mountain Dog.

THE FUTURE

The modern standardized Caucasian Mountain Dog continues his partnership with mankind as an estate and ranch guardian and family companion. In the US, efforts are underway to place dogs on sheep ranches in hopes of restoring the breed's age-old agricultural role. Aboriginal Caucasian dogs, bred for flock and family protection, can still be found throughout the Caucasus. The Armenia Kennel Club has written a separate breed standard for their local dogs, which they call "Gampr." One day we may see different cultivated versions of the Caucasian dogs from different regions of the Caucasus competing at exhibitions under breed names separate from Caucasian Mountain Dog.

Even the strongest, most robust dogs need to rest sometimes!

CAUCASIAN MOUNTAIN DOG

"That's not a dog, it's a bear!" is the comment Caucasian Mountain Dog owners hear most often when they walk their dogs down the road. Curious awestruck motorists will stop their cars to ask if it really is a dog or which breed of dog it is that has caught their attention. The large size, seemingly even more immense because of the attractive long heavy coat and the substantial head with high-set bluntly cropped ears, wide muzzle and noticeable cheekbones conjure up the image of a wild animal more than one of a domesticated dog.

Breed lovers extol the virtues of the Caucasian Mountain Dog. We describe a dog of great self-esteem that is always aware of his power, utilizing a keen intelligence that evaluates a situation with an attentive gaze. Protection is the job of the Caucasian Mountain Dog. An owner entrusts this dog with his own life, the lives of his family and the security of his property. The owner depends upon the breed to be naturally protective without specific training for the task, and to be gentle

and loving with family members and children.

Molded by the forces of nature in the often harsh working conditions of the Caucasus Mountains, the Caucasian Mountain Dog is a product of both natural selection and man's ever-changing demands for the various tasks that the breed has had to perform over many generations. Recognition of the original guardian role for which the Caucasian Mountain Dog was developed provides a better understanding of the breed's characteristics and behavior today.

A PHYSICALLY ROBUST BREED
While each family will vary in the care and keeping of a dog, the working Caucasian Mountain Dog often lives half-wild in the Caucasus Mountains. Historically, no custom of selling dogs exists in the Caucasus, and the pups born to the working dogs are needed to replenish the family guardian pack or are traded to neighboring herdsmen. Excess litters are considered an unnecessary burden. Therefore a herdsman may keep five or six dogs, of

which four are males and only one or two are females. Bitches cycle every eight to eleven months. Male dogs will battle for the breeding rights to the bitch in season, with the winning male siring the litter. Puppies are usually whelped in an outdoor lair with minimal human intervention and care. The herdsman may leave only the male puppies and destroy all but one or two of the females. About 20% of the mountain-born puppies actually live to adulthood. Herdsmen crop the puppies' ears horizontally and bluntly, close to the head (in theory to prevent their later loss to a predatory wolf) without the use of anesthesia. A difficult mountain life begins from birth for the Caucasian Mountain Dog, governed by the principle of "survival of the fittest."

The flock migration from summer to winter pasture may span miles. Only sound, healthy dogs can complete the journey. Predator attacks are frequent, and only the strongest and most efficient guardians that meet these challenges live to reproduce. Food rations are meager. The dogs are fed a cornmeal- or bread-based diet, and sometimes a little goat's milk. Only dogs that are "easy-keepers" with the instinct to supplement their diets by hunting rodents and rabbits endure.

Over the centuries, the Caucasian Mountain Dog breed

developed physical characteristics advantageous to living and working in the Caucasus Mountains environment. The breed's thick double coat and mane-like ruff are insulation from heat and cold and protection from predator bites. The coat has a characteristic oiliness with water-repellent and tangle-resistant properties, and an odor that serves as a scent warning to predators. Dirt that dries on the coat shakes off. Dogs at higher elevations developed longer coats in response to colder winter

Traditionally, ears are cropped close to the head. Cropping is done on pups at a very young age.

A representative of the breed from Germany, which differs somewhat from the dogs in Russia.

weather, and larger chest and lung capacity in response to thinner air. Dogs in the steppe regions are often shorter-coated in response to the more temperate climate.

Conditions in the Soviet-run kennels were less extreme than mountain conditions. Kennel Caucasian Mountain Dogs were well fed until perestroika and did not face animal predators. However, natural selection was replaced by a half-century of human selection in these kennels. Dogs that could not perform their government guarding service were destroyed, and only the largest, strongest, most aggressive dogs were chosen for breeding.

Today's Caucasian Mountain Dog is heir to the robust, healthy constitution of his mountain

Regardless of type, a Caucasian must be sound, robust and healthy overall.

flock-guardian ancestors. The breed's most significant health problem is a high incidence of radiographic hip and elbow dysplasia, for which all breeding stock should be screened. However, the breed is so physically strong and stoic that few individuals are crippled from these diseases. Entropion (turning in of the eyelids) also occurs in the breed with some frequency. Hypothyroidism, seizures, food allergies, gastric torsion, heart problems and early cancers that plague other dog breeds are reported occasionally but are not widespread in the general population. Average life expectancy is about ten years, of course with some living longer, and the breed stays hardy in its senior years.

Do You Know about Hip Dysplasia?

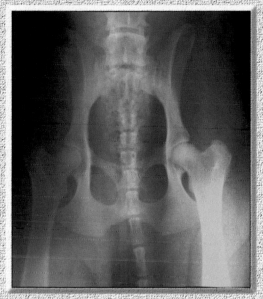

X-ray of a dog with "Good" hips.

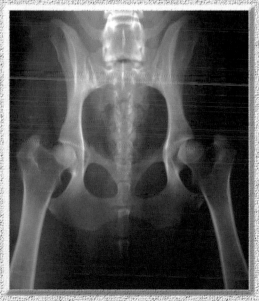

X-ray of a dog with "Moderate" dysplastic hips.

Hip dysplasia is a fairly common condition found in pure-bred dogs. When a dog has hip dysplasia, his hind leg has an incorrectly formed hip joint. By constant use of the hip joint, it becomes more and more loose, wears abnormally and may become arthritic.

Hip dysplasia can only be confirmed with an x-ray, but certain symptoms may indicate a problem. Your dog may have a hip dysplasia problem if he walks in a peculiar manner, hops instead of smoothly runs, uses his hind legs in unison (to keep the pressure off the weak joint), has trouble getting up from a prone position or always sits with both legs together on one side of his body.

As the dog matures, he may adapt well to life with a bad hip, but in a few years the arthritis develops and many dogs with hip dysplasia become crippled.

Hip dysplasia is considered an inherited disease and only can be diagnosed definitively by x-ray when the dog is two years old, although symptoms often appear earlier. Some experts claim that a special diet might help your puppy outgrow the bad hip, but the usual treatments are surgical. The removal of the pectineus muscle, the removal of the round part of the femur, reconstructing the pelvis and replacing the hip with an artificial one are all surgical interventions that are expensive, but they are usually very successful. Follow the advice of your veterinarian.

TERRITORIAL GUARDIANS

The Caucasian Mountain Dog, like other flock-guardian breeds, is territorially protective. Instinctively, he considers whatever belongs within his territory to be his private property and thinks in terms of "my house," "my owner," "my car." The breed is innately distrustful of strangers, new situations and any changes in the environment. In the Caucasus, the dogs bond with livestock and patrol the large areas of grazing land. The dogs defend the livestock from predators and keep out the thieves. The breed guards the flock with other Caucasian Mountain Dogs, working as a team in a pack hierarchy.

The choice of grazing land is weather-controlled and subject to winter snows, rainy-season floods and drought. Herdsmen move the sheep and cattle safely and efficiently in response to weather conditions and between winter and summer pastures. The dogs are required to quickly adapt to their new surroundings and commence guarding duty wherever the flock is pastured.

Caucasian Mountain Dogs bred by the Soviet government army for guarding factories and installations were selected for this territorial guarding instinct. Today the modern Caucasian Mountain Dog kept as a working companion dog retains a strong "sense of

At only six months old, this youngster already looks alert, keen and strong.

space." Dogs of correct temperament will begin guarding an area after being there for only a short time and will almost immediately guard an object placed in their care. In keeping with the territorial-guarding nature, the Caucasian Mountain Dog tends to be fiercely protective at home and indifferent to non-threatening events and strangers "off property" if they are properly socialized to understand the difference.

DISCERNING GUARDIANS
Constantly engaging the predator would probably have resulted in a dog that died young of infection from bite wounds. Thus the herdsman kept dogs that could scare off the predator most of the time and have to actually bite only when necessary. This process is not dissimilar from the decision process used by the wolf. An injured predator cannot hunt any more effectively than an injured guardian dog can protect.

While guarding the flock, the Caucasian Mountain Dog attempts to deter predators from entering the protected area. The dogs urinate and defecate on the outer perimeter of the territory so their scent will discourage the predator from a distance. Because attacks occur more often at night, the Caucasian Mountain Dog rests during the day and keeps a night vigil. Patrolling the territory

perimeter, the dogs will bark a steady warble warning into the night to let any potential predators know that a sentry is on duty.

When a predator is in fact detected, the Caucasian Mountain Dog has a graduated display of protective behaviors. The bark increases to sound the alarm, alerting the herdsman to potential danger and communicating to the flock to group together. The dogs place themselves between the flock and the approaching threat, and they growl and bark with increasing ferocity: "Stop or I will stop you."

If the predator threat persists, the Caucasian dog team will divide their duties of protection. The alpha dog may range out, identifying the threat more precisely, with the balance of the dog team staying back to concentrate on thwarting attempts to

True to the breed's heritage, Caucasian Mountain Dogs of all ages take to livestock instantly.

Taiga Esquire, a five-month-old bitch puppy bred and owned by the author, shows her budding guard-dog skills by "sounding the alarm."

scatter the flock and isolate sheep. In these extreme incidences, when the dogs are certain that the intruders will not be deterred and there is an actual life threat to the flock, the alpha dog will attack the alpha wolf, fighting to the death in silence. The adult Caucasian Mountain Dog is capable of killing an adult wolf if necessary.

Possibly as a result of the Soviet-run kennel breeding selections, or the poor breeding practices during perestroika, not all individuals of the modern Caucasian Mountain Dog breed today exhibit naturally discriminating judgment, the ability to discern true threat from benign interference. Not all individuals use only necessary force when guarding. While the best of modern breeding works toward a breed-wide stable guardian temperament, a few individuals in the breed today are unduly aggressive and require extra measures of socialization and control to keep them safely in society.

INDEPENDENT THINKERS

Unlike the Rottweiler and German Shepherd, the Caucasian Mountain Dog has not been bred specifically for obedience to man as his fellow guard-dog breeds have. Whether the Rottweiler was droving cattle or pulling the butcher's wagon, or the German Shepherd was herding sheep or protecting an army base, these breeds looked to man regularly for direction and acted according to the master's command. On the contrary, the Caucasus herdsmen bred dogs to work in close proximity to them and to be mindful of them, but to be independent-minded enough to perform their job without direction if necessary. When the hungry wolf pack pounced upon the flock, the Caucasian Mountain Dog did not have time to look over his shoulder to see what the herdsman wanted him to do. The dog had to assess the situation for himself, take action and dispatch the threat without hesitation or delay.

LOW PREY DRIVE AND GENTLE NURTURING SIDE

While adolescent flock-guardian dogs will chase stock in play and require human supervision, the adult Caucasian Mountain Dog is often left alone with the sheep and the lambs he protects. While he will hunt rabbits and rodents when hungry, the Caucasian Mountain Dog, like other flock-guardian breeds, has a low "prey drive," which is the instinct to chase, triggered by sight. The dogs move calmly and slowly so as not to frighten the livestock. So accepted by the flock are they that they will often be involved in the birthing process and lick newborn sheep and goats. During the winter season, the dogs accompany the flocks back to the village territories and have to interact gently and patiently with the village women and children. Individual dogs exhibiting undue aggression toward the family or other villagers are often destroyed.

Within the context of our modern world, Caucasian Mountain Dogs should be able to adapt and get along with livestock, other pets and children, provided they are raised and socialized properly and understand their role in the pack hierarchy. The breed can be quarrelsome with other dogs in the pack, especially of the same sex when vying for alpha dominance. Strange dogs encountered on the street often invoke an aggressive reaction from Caucasian Mountain Dogs unless the dogs have been carefully socialized to this situation.

INSTINCTIVE BEHAVIORS

Modern Caucasian Mountain Dogs retain strong instinctive behaviors of their mountain ancestors. Like wild canids, they will dig to reach water, to build a den for warmth in the winter and to reach the cooler ground in the summer. Dams will dig birthing dens and sometimes prefer to whelp outside. They will regurgitate food and water into the mouths of their pups when weaning.

The Caucasian Mountain Dog tends to be a homebody with a strong sense of territory. However, the breed has tendencies to want to expand the protected area over to neighboring properties. They can be aggressive toward and injure or kill neighborhood dogs that are viewed in the same category as predators, and they can attack strangers or anything in the

The Caucasian Mountain Dog is a natural guardian of home and family whose territorial instinct sometimes can extend to what's on the other side of the fence.

area perceived as a threat. The Caucasian Mountain Dog is a clever escape artist. Individuals of this breed can dig under and scale over fences and figure out how to open gate latches with their bear-like paws. Chaining out will frustrate the dog and encourage inappropriate aggression, and is not recommended for the breed. Secure 6-foot fencing is required with hotwire reinforcement as necessary.

TRAINING AND SOCIALIZATION

Caucasian Mountain Dogs are generally easy to get along with, but basic training, proper raising from puppyhood and consistent socialization are essential. The Caucasian Mountain Dog views his family as a pack with established social positions, including a leader. If the Caucasian perceives a vacancy in the pack-leader position, the dog will assume the leadership role. Dogs of this breed may be very cooperative during times of normal activity but will "take charge" if there is any disruption in routine, such as a visit to the vet or a stranger on the property.

Successful breed ownership requires that the owner maintain the leadership or alpha role at all times. Puppies need extensive handling and must learn to be comfortable with being picked up and held, having their ears cleaned and having their owners handle their food bowls during meals. Young Caucasians must be rewarded for positive behavior, which nurtures the dog's acceptance and trust of his owner as the leader. The Caucasian Mountain Dog must learn to trust the alpha owner's decisions. Inappropriate behavior, especially any aggressive or dominant behavior toward family members or pets, must be corrected firmly and consistently.

The Caucasian Mountain Dog breed innately views the world suspiciously. Therefore all puppy dealings with the world must be pleasant. Caucasian puppies should be touched and petted by kind strangers and never be abused or scared. Puppies should be socialized off the family's property two or three times per week, encountering as many new situations as possible. Puppies should also see strangers on their home property at weekly intervals and learn that visitors are part of the normal routine. The Caucasian Mountain Dog requires continued socialization to people on and off property throughout his life, so as not to become overly territorial and unmanageable.

Caucasian Mountain Dogs benefit from attending obedience classes for basic training. The dogs learn good manners and also gain valuable experience by meeting and obeying simple commands around strange people and dogs. Caucasian Mountain Dogs

"I know I'm good-looking, but you don't have to stare!"

are very intelligent and learn quickly, but they become bored easily, especially with repetitive training methods. Short sessions utilizing a blend of traditional and inductive training methods are most productive.

A BREED NOT FOR EVERYONE
The Caucasian Mountain Dog's breed characteristics, indispensable to the herdsmen of the Caucasus for thousands of years, are the same characteristics that make the breed perfect for some modern situations but very unsuitable for many average pet homes. Since the breed has low "prey drive," Caucasians are generally not interested in playing ball with the family children.

Caucasian Mountain Dogs need sufficient exercise and a job to do, so they are best kept by home-owners with acreage to guard. This breed is not well suited for apartment living. The requirement of secure 6-foot fencing is a very cost-prohibitive consideration of ownership. The dog's den-digging behavior can tear up a flower garden or a carpet, and his nocturnal barking behavior can strain neighbor relations and violate noise ordinances. The breed can have difficulties exercising appropriate judgment in our complex modern society where delivery men who carry strange-looking packages to the front door are not to be considered a threat. The owner must keep his dog under complete control at all times. The Caucasian Mountain Dog requires an above-average amount of time and owner commitment invested in socialization to teach the dog about the human world around him so that he does not overreact to normal everyday situations. Because the Caucasian Mountain Dog is an independent worker who will take charge on his own initiative, this is not a breed that can be expected to be reliably obedient off leash in public. The Caucasian Mountain Dog can run off to investigate something in a blink of an eye, and he will. If he perceives something as threatening, he will rely on his own judgment, disobeying his owner deliberately until he has handled the threat his way.

The Caucasian is loyal and loving to his family, forming a strong bond with those who raise him.

A Caucasian Mountain Dog can be a girl's best friend!

THE COMPANION CAUCASIAN MOUNTAIN DOG

Owning a Caucasian Mountain Dog is like owning a piece of nature. For the dedicated breed fanciers who are enamored with the self-thinking, instinctual and protective character of the Caucasian Mountain Dog breed, and who have the time and resources to correctly raise and socialize and keep this powerful guardian breed safely, the Caucasian Mountain Dog is indeed an excellent choice for a compelling canine companion. At once loyal and loving, the Caucasian Mountain Dog enjoys the company of his owners and is especially suited for outdoor farm life and activities such as hiking and swimming. He makes a terrific best friend, fearless and faithful, always willing and able to stand by and defend his owners in every situation, as the breed has done throughout the centuries.

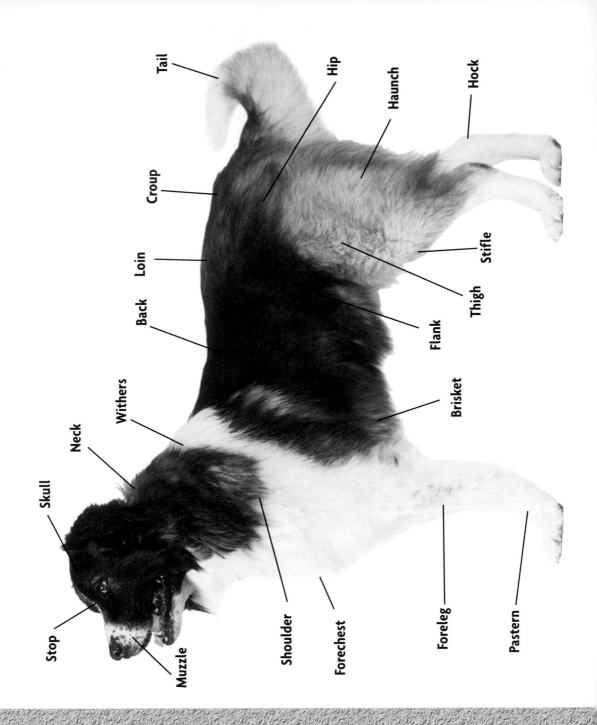

Tail

Hip

Haunch

Hock

Croup

Loin

Back

Stifle

Thigh

Flank

Withers

Brisket

Neck

Skull

Stop

Muzzle

Shoulder

Forechest

Foreleg

Pastern

EXTERNAL FEATURES OF THE CAUCASIAN MOUNTAIN DOG

CAUCASIAN MOUNTAIN DOG

INTRODUCTION TO THE BREED STANDARD

A breed standard is a modern convention, describing an ideal dog of a breed as envisioned by a group of people at a particular point in history. A breed standard guides breeding toward a predictable genetic package so that the dog breed successfully fits a niche. Breed standards often change in response to social needs, fashion and fad, and the Caucasian Mountain Dog breed standard is no exception.

Cynological research historically described "types" of Caucasian Mountain Dogs that differed in conformation because of different geographic conditions and isolation, herdsman preferences and possibly local inbreeding. Generally the breed was divided into two groups: the heavier, larger-boned, longer-coated Mountain or Trans-Caucasian type and the smaller, leggier, shorter-coated Steppe type. Within these groups were several distinguishable subtypes or regional varieties, including Georgian type, Armenian type, Azerbaijan type and Dagestan type, each of which differed in some significant way in general appearance, coat length and color. From the aboriginal flock-guardian dogs, bred in a range of sizes, colors and body types, only for working ability and not for "conformation," to the Soviet guard dog, bred to be huge, ferocious and of almost any color and coat length, to today's modern cultivated breed, uniformly beautiful with its bear-like head, long plush coat and preferably solid color, the breed standard of perfection for the ideal Caucasian Mountain Dog has undergone significant changes during the past century.

The Caucasian Mountain Dog is currently classified as a Fédération Cynologique Internationale (FCI) Group 2 Molossoid Breed of Mountain Type. The first Caucasian Mountain Dog breed standard was published in 1931. In 1952, the Trans-Caucasian and the Steppe Caucasian were identified by the USSR Kennel Club as two separate breeds. In 1976, a modern standard reclassified the

Russkiy Medved Onega, a bitch at ten months of age.

Caucasian Mountain Dog as one breed. Updates to the standard regarding the bite and teeth were added in 1982. Since the demise of the USSR, and the 1995 FCI recognition of the Russian Kynological Federation (RKF), the Russian National Breed Club standard is in the process of being unified with the FCI breed standard. In 1997, the Russian National Breed Club ratified a newly revised Caucasian Mountain Dog breed standard, which fanciers expect will be approved by the FCI.

The first Soviet/Russian Caucasian Mountain Dog breed standards, although based on the physical specifications of the Georgian type dogs, allowed for a fairly wide range of physical

characteristics. Dogs judged in the same conformation ring often did not look like the same breed in a modern cookie-cutter sense. Breeding selection placed performance characteristics ahead of strictly "conformation" or "breed points" in importance. Dogs exhibiting physical differences resulting from geographical conditions (e.g., Mountain type vs. Steppe type) were accepted. Area-guarding ability, size and ferocity were emphasized and deemed essential. Lack of working temperament was severely penalized. The cultivation of the most ferocious-looking black-masked solid-colored dogs occurred. Under the Soviet regime, the breed standard reflected the social needs of a guardian dog used for territorial protection of factories and military facilities.

The modern Caucasian Mountain Dog breed standard is based on a narrower interpretation of the correct Georgian type of Caucasian Mountain Dog, which calls for a large-boned, powerful and strong dog, with a long, coarse coat, preferably with a black mask and solid coat color. The 1997 Russian National Breed Club-ratified breed standard memorialized the favored black-masked dogs in solid shades over pintos and piebald.

The distinguishing feature of the modern Caucasian Mountain

Dog breed standard is the tremendous emphasis on the bear-like head, which must be large, especially in males. It is important for the modern Caucasian Mountain Dog to have medium-sized deep-set dark eyes, with the expression of great will, self confidence, cleverness and distrust. High-set cropped ears are placed on a very wide skull with well-developed cheekbones and a strong muzzle, slightly shorter than the skull.

Russian National Breed Club President and breed judge Galina Kirkitskaya sums up the importance of the head as follows: "First while judging, I examine all dogs, dividing them into two groups in my mind. The first group includes dogs that have a standard head. 'The breed is in the head' is a more convenient motto of Caucasians' assessment that English breeders use. I'm of the same opinion. For instance, a dog that is not proportionally built and of wrong gait, but with a beautiful properly built head is a Caucasian that has not a properly built body, not so good gait. A proportionally built dog with excellent gait and a head unlike that of a Caucasian is an excellent dog of another breed. So, it cannot be assessed as a Caucasian. This is the fundamental point for a Caucasian's assessment. A dog with a beautiful head may get the low rating if it

has severe deviations from the breed standard. But only the proper type, that is a beautiful standard head, is the basic point in judging."

The current FCI breed standard requires a minimum height of 65 cm (25.5 inches) for dogs and 62 cm (24.5 inches) for bitches. The breed standard adopted by the Russian National Breed Club favors a taller dog, with an increased minimum height of 68 cm (26.75 inches) for dogs and 64 cm (25 inches) for bitches, preferring 72 to 75 cm (almost 28.5 to 29.5 inches) for dogs and 66 to 69 cm (almost 26 to a little over 27 inches) for bitches. Weight is not specified in the current FCI breed standard.

Russkiy Medved Onega, a bit more mature at 19 months of age.

Well-developed bone structure and very strong musculature are required by each of the modern standards. To express proportions of height to bone size, the Soviet Kennel Club began utilizing measurements and ratios called indexes, which are still used today. This was thought very useful, since the breed standard has never specified a height limit. To calculate the "Index of Bone," the height at the withers is divided by the circumference of the metacarpus times 100. The bone index of bitches is higher because of the lower height.

The ideal body is slightly longer than tall, powerful, deep and wide with a well-sprung brisket and a wide chest. The back is wide with a level topline and powerful loin. Angulation is moderate. While standing, the Caucasian Mountain Dog's hind legs should not brace backwards. The ideal gait is free with spring off the pasterns, changing from a short trot to a heavy Molosser-like gallop with acceleration. The tail is long, held low in repose and carried high when the dog is alert or moving.

The double coat must be thick, straight and off-standing, with characteristic feathering on the tail and hind legs. The FCI breed standard describes three coat lengths: long, medium and short. The Russian National Breed Club standard describes only two coat lengths. Many coat shades are described, except for solid black and solid brown, which are disqualified under the current FCI and RKF breed standards. Full dentition and scissors bite are required. The Russian National Breed Club breed standard revision describes the temperament simply as confident, even and calm.

Following is the current Caucasian Mountain Dog FCI breed standard and the proposed Russian National Breed Club standard awaiting FCI approval. The dogs of Russia, where the largest breed population is found, are judged by the Russian standard, while the rest of Europe's Caucasians are judged by the FCI standard. While this author is in love with the cultivated bear-like Caucasian Mountain Dog of Russia, it is my concern that, as the Caucasian Mountain Dog is further standardized into a huge-headed, beautiful companion dog, swinging the pendulum away from the ferocious Soviet army "chain-dog," too much emphasis will be placed on a "pretty face" without attention to working territorial temperament. I fear that selection toward even more massive size will be at the sacrifice of athletic ability. The Caucasian Mountain Dog's breed history has clearly demonstrated that beauty, athleticism and working ability are not mutually exclusive, and future Caucasian Mountain Dog breeders must carefully breed for all of these traits.

FCI STANDARD FOR THE CAUCASIAN SHEPHERD DOG

Other names: Kavkazskaya Ovcharka, Caucasian Ovcharka, Caucasian Sheepdog, Tatar Shepherd Dog, Caucasian Mountain Dog.

FCI Classification: #328, Group 2, Section 2.

Land of Origin: Russia, Georgia, Armenia, Azerbaijani Union Republics, Karbardino-Balkan, Daghestan and the Kalmykia autonomous republics.

General Description: The Caucasian Shepherd Dogs are a little larger than medium-sized dogs with a strong build; their nature is fierce and they are

Ch. Frol Gvidonovich Svetlogo Doma, a three-year-old male.

distrustful of strangers. These characteristics, and in addition, their stamina, understanding nature and ability to adapt to the most varied weather conditions, make it possible for Caucasian Shepherd Dogs to live in almost all of the climatic regions of the former USSR. Caucasian Shepherd Dogs are found mostly in Georgia, Armenia, Azerbaijani Union Republics, Karbardino-Balkan, Daghestan and the Kalmykia autonomous republics. Further in the Steppes of the North Caucasus and in the area of Astrakan. In the Trans-Caucasus areas, the dogs are heavier; in the Steppes area, on the contrary, lighter, long legged, often short-haired.

General Appearance: Powerful appearance with solid structure and strong musculature. The skin is thick but elastic.
    Minor faults: Somewhat too slight or bloated (spongy) physique.

Major faults: Too slight or bloated physique.

Bone Index-Density: Height of the withers divided by the circumference of the wrist. Males: 21 cm to 22 cm. Bitches: 20 cm to 22 cm.
Minor faults: Slight deviation from the cited index.
Major faults: Severe deviations from the given size.

Size Index-Format: Shall not exceed 108 or be below 102.
Minor faults: Slight deviation from the cited index.
Major faults: Severe deviations from the given size.

Height at Withers: The male dog must not be under 65 cm. The bitch not under 62 cm.
Major faults: Height at the withers under 65 cm for males and under 62 cm for bitches.

Character: Strong, balanced, calm nature. Revealing a good defense reaction which will be used if necessary. Typically ferocious towards and distrustful of strangers.
Minor faults: Lethargy. Friendly or trusting towards strangers.
Major faults: Timid, cowardice. A great deal of apathy. Not ferocious.

Gender Type: Well revealed. Males are larger and more solid. Bitches are smaller and have a slighter build.

Minor faults: Only a slight deviation in gender type. Bitches fit the model of males.

Major faults: Strong deviation in gender type. Males fit the model of bitches. Cryptorchid, monorchid.

Coat: The fur is natural, coarse with strongly developed lighter undercoat. On the head and on the front sides of the limbs, the hair is shorter and close-fitting. The coat is divided into three types. Long-haired: With long top hair. The long hairs form a mane on the haunch. With well-developed pants, especially on the back sides of the leg, feathering. Shorthaired: With thick relatively short hair without mane. Without feathers on the haunch, underside or the leg and tail. A variety which is a cross between the above-mentioned types: Longhaired but without mane, feathers on haunch, underside and without the bushy tail.

Major faults: Fine wavy hair. Without undercoat.

Color: Various grays. Mostly light to rust-colored tones. Also rust-colored, straw, yellow, white, earth-colored, striped, but also spotted and piebald.

Major faults: Black, black flecked and brown colors in various combinations.

Head study of crop-eared dog of pleasing type, proportion and substance.

Head: Solid with a wide skull and strongly developed bones. Wide flat forehead which is bisected by a slight furrow. The progression from the forehead to the area of the muzzle is slight. The muzzle is shorter than the forehead, and is slightly tapered with strong but tightly closed dry lips. The nose is large, wide and black. It is permissible for the nose to be brown if the particular dog or bitch has a white or light-colored face.

Minor faults: The head is not sufficiently wide or solid. Too strongly domed or too steep or too flat in the forehead. Short or elongated nose. Lips that are not firmly closed and do not hang over.

Russkiy Medved Ladoga, a four-year-old bitch.

Major faults: Slight small head with pointed muzzle. Not corresponding to the physique. Snub nose.

Ears: Hanging. Set high. Always cropped short.
Minor faults: Low set. Not cropped ears.

Eyes: Dark. Medium-large. Oval-shaped, set deep.
Minor faults: Light-colored eyes. Slightly hanging bottom lids. Eye disease.
Major faults: Different-colored eyes. Hanging bottom eyelids which partially reveal sclera.

Teeth: White, large, well-developed teeth which should lie tightly next to each other. The base of the incisors are lined up. Scissors grip.
Minor faults: Wear and tear of the teeth does not correspond to the age of the dog. Broken teeth, which however do not hinder a proper scissors bite. Loss of no

more than the two first premolars or one of the second premolars. Light yellow color.
Major faults: Small light underdeveloped teeth. Incisors not lined up. Loss of a third or fourth premolar, or of a molar. Teeth with strongly damaged enamel.

Neck: Very powerful and short. Is not carried high but at an angle of 30–40 degrees to the line of the back.
Minor faults: Longer neck. Neck that is weak.

Chest: Broad, deep, somewhat domed. The bottom line reaches the height of the elbow.
Minor faults: Somewhat flattened out chest. The bottom line does not reach the height of the elbow.
Major faults: A flat narrow underdeveloped chest.

Abdomen: Moderate tuck-up.
Minor faults: Too strongly tucked up or hanging abdomen.

Withers: Very wide. Muscular and very clearly separated from the back.
Minor faults: Weakly developed, which is not separated from the back.

Back: Very wide, straight, muscular.
Minor faults: A weak or dome-shaped or slimmer back.

Major faults: Long, sagging or humpbacked small of the back.

Croup: Wide, muscular, almost horizontal.
   Minor faults: Not muscular enough. A croup that drops off.
   Major faults: Slim, short, or a croup that drops off strongly.

Tail: Set high. If hanging, reaches the ankle joint. Able to curl itself or be hook-shaped. Tail should not be cropped.

Front Limbs: Standing and seen from the front, straight and parallel to each other. The shoulder and upper arm angle comes to 100 degrees. Upper arms are straight, solid, moderately long. The pasterns short, solid, standing vertically and only giving slightly. The length of the forelimbs to the elbow comes somewhat over half the height of the withers. Long-legged index 50–54.
   Minor faults: Small differences regarding the shoulder angle. Somewhat shortened or elongated forearm. Elbows that turn slightly outward. Feet turned slightly outward while walking. Too strongly curved pastern.
   Major faults: Straight or pointed shoulders. Crooked or too slim forearms. Elbows which jut strongly outward. Throwing out of the feet toward the outside

while walking. Bowlegged, one or both front legs.

Hind Limbs: Standing and seen from behind, straight and parallel to each other. Seen from the side, knee joint somewhat stretched out. Short lower leg. Powerful ankle joints which are wide and somewhat stretched. The metatarsus solid. While standing, hind limbs should not brace backwards. A vertical line should run from the buttocks towards the middle of the ankle joints and the metacarpus.
   Minor faults: When viewed from behind, not completely parallel. Standing hind limbs that are slightly knock kneed or bowlegged, or legs that are wide

The Caucasian's legs are strong and solid, his feet are large and rounded and his tail can be held in a curl.

Ch. Frol Gvidonovich iz Svetlogo Doma, a three-year-old male.

apart or too close together in a standing position. Too flat or too high a backside.

Major faults: Strong deviation from being parallel. Totally straight backside, bowlegged, backside too high.

Paws: Large oval form, domed and well closed.

Minor faults: Weak or too-stretched-out paws.

Major faults: Spread out toes or flat paws.

Gait: Free, usually even calm gallop. A typical gait is a short trot which breaks into a somewhat ungainly gallop with acceleration. The limbs must move in a parallel manner in a straight line, whereby the front legs tend to move towards the middle. The joints of the front and back limbs stretch slightly. The back and the small of the back spring smoothly. The withers and the croup should stay on one level while trotting.

Minor faults: Deviation from normal gait (turning inward or outward). Not stretching joints enough. No smooth movement of the back and small of the back while trotting. Raised croup. Slight swinging of the croup. Swinging with the buttocks.

Major faults: Inhibited. Clumsy gait while trotting. In comparison, croup carried high to the withers. Brusque on- and- off of the croup while trotting. Ambling.

Disqualifying Faults:
• Any deviations from the solely permissible scissors bite.
• Cryptorchid. One side or both sides.
• Underdeveloped prostate glands.
• Black or brown coloration.
• Loss of a canine tooth or incisor.
• Loss of a third or fourth premolar or a molar.

Note: Male dogs must show two visibly normal testicles which lie well in the scrotum.

RUSSIAN NATIONAL BREED CLUB STANDARD
Kavkazskaya Ovcharka—Standard 328. Adopted by the Russian Kynological Federation 1997.

Brief Historical Essay: The Kavkazskaya Ovcharka is one of the ancient breeds, it descends from the Mastiff-like dogs of Tibet that are related by their origin to the shepherd and fighting dogs of Asia. For many years these fine dogs accompanied the cattle-breeders on the vast territories that stretched from the Caucasus steppes and foothills to the Plateau of Iran. Mostly this breed has been formed in the severe mountain conditions.

General Appearance: A large dog of the rough-built type, with massive bone and strong, well-developed musculature. The format is slightly long. The sex type is clearly defined—the males are larger, more massive, with the heavier, larger heads, with a long mane.
Faults: Dry or loose build, poor bone, square or too long body. Well-marked underchest.

Character/Behavior: Behavior is bold, balanced, quiet. Unconfident behavior and excessive excitability are not characteristic of the breed.

Main Proportions: The minimum height for males is 68 cm, for females 64 cm. If a dog is proportionally built, it should be more. The ratio of the muzzle length to the skull length is 2:3. A dog mustn't seem leggy or cobby.

Head: Large, massive.
Faults: Small, light, unproportional. Domed forehead; sloped

occiput. Long, weak, pinched, rather broken up or down muzzle, a weak lower jaw. Abrupt stop. Skin wrinkles on the head. Jowls. Haw eyes.

Skull: A broad and well-developed skull with strong jaws. A broad forehead, slightly domed, with a shallow long furrow and marked, but not prominent supra-orbital ridges.

Stop: Not long, well marked, but not abrupt.

Muzzle: Massive, of a great depth, blunt, well-filled under the eyes and in the set region, gradually pointed to the nose.

Muzzle Length: Slightly shorter than the length of the skull. Lips thick, tight.

Nose: Big, black; the light-fawn and white dogs can have light noses.

Teeth: Full dentition (42 teeth). White, large, well-developed, tightly set. The incisors' bases are set in a line. A scissors bite or level bite in spite of age.
Faults: Small, widely spaced, rather broken teeth.

Eyes: Not big, oval, dark, set obliquely, deeply and well apart. The eyelids are close fitting.
Faults: Very big, protruding, round, very light blue or goose-

berry color. Haw eyes, a well-developed third eyelid.

Ears: Hanging on the ear cartilages, not big, set on high, short-cropped.

Neck: Strong, slightly shorter than the head length, crested, set at an angle of 30–40 degrees to a back line. A slight dewlap is admissible.
Fault: High-set.

Body: As follows
Topline: The well-marked and well-developed withers, wide, muscular, slightly higher than a back line. A wide, straight, strong muscular back.
Fault: A narrow, sway or roach back.

Loin: Short, wide, muscular, slightly arched.
Faults: Narrow, long, arched or sagging.

Croup: Wide, muscular, average long, rounded, nearly horizontal.
Faults: Narrow, short, sunken. Croup that is rather higher than the withers.

Chest: Lowered to the elbow line or lower, long, broad, rounded in section. The ribs are definitely arched; the false ribs are well developed. The front part of the chest is slightly prominent in comparison with the gleno-humeral joints.

Faults: Underdeveloped, flat, narrow, shallow, short.

Belly: Reasonably tucked-up.

Tail: High-set, dropped when a dog is quiet, reaches the hock joints. Sickle curved, hooked or curled.

Forequarters: At front view straight, wide and parallel set. The blades and shoulder bones are long, make an angle of the glenohumeral joint of about 100 degrees. The length of the forelegs up to the elbows is a bit longer or just the same as the half of dog's height in withers. The long-legged index is 50 or a bit higher.
Fault: Narrow front.

Forearms: Straight, massive, rounded in section, muscular, average long. The elbows are turned backwards.
Faults: Upright or protruding upper arms; short, cabriole or delicate forearms. Weak elbows.

Pasterns: Short, massive, nearly upright.
Faults: Knuckling, weak pasterns.

Hindquarters: At rear view, straight and parallel; at side view, slightly straight in stifle and in hock. The hindquarters are not chopped off behind.
Faults: Angulation that is too

FAULTS IN PROFILE

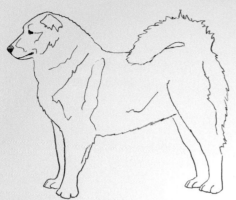
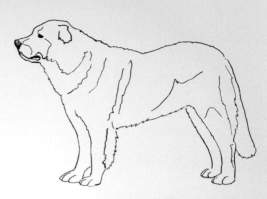

LEFT: Toes out in front, high in rear, very straight behind. This tail carriage is acceptable when the dog is moving or particularly alert or excited. **RIGHT:** Too long and low, too heavy, loose jowls, upright shoulders, poor topline, high in rear, lacking angulation behind.

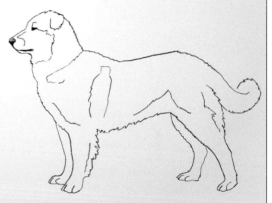

LEFT: Generally lacking substance and strength, muzzle too long, narrow in both front and rear, soft topline, very straight behind. **RIGHT:** Ewe-necked, upright shoulders, toes out in front, soft topline, long back, high in rear, steep croup, cowhocked, lacking substance and strength, weak pasterns.

marked or straight; hindquarters that are chopped off behind; weak ligaments.

Upper and Lower Thighs: Not long, strong and wide hock joints, little angulation.
Fault: Sickle hocks.

Rear Pasterns: Massive, upright rear pasterns.

Feet: Big, circular, arched, cat-like.
Faults: Flat, splay.

Movement: Free, usually unhurried. The characteristic feature is

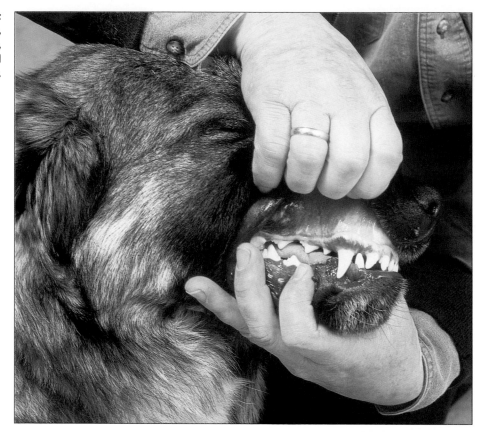

a not-stretching trot that changes into a slightly heavy gallop when speeding up. The legs must move straight forward, the forequarters should move on the middle line. The joints of the fore- and hindquarters unbend freely. When trotting, the withers and the croup are on the same level, the topline is level.

Faults: Stretching trot, too-reachy action that is not characteristic of the breed. Bindy, heavy gait. Too high in croup when moving. Unbalanced movement. Uncorrected pace.

Skin: Thick, rather elastic.

Coat Hair: Straight, coarse, with dense undercoat. On the head and on the front sides of the legs, the hair is shorter and taut. Depending on the hair length, they distinguish two coat types: Long-haired—with long outer hair. Long hair makes a "mane" on a neck, feathers and "bridges" on the rear

A prize-winning Caucasian Mountain Dog at the World Dog Show held in Milan, Italy in 2000.

sides of the legs. Long hair covering the tail makes it thick and furry. Short-haired—with dense, rather short hair. There are no "mane," feathers and falling hair on the tail. The hair is off-standing, about 4 cm in length on the loin.

Color: Various: Gray—from dark gray, nearly black, to light-fawn-gray, including partly gray; red—from dark red-brown to light fawn, including partly red; white; brindle—from dark brown-brindle, nearly black, to light fawn-brindle. When one color, there may be a black mask, white patching on the chest, the belly, on the legs and on the tail tip. There are piebald and spotted colors of the mentioned tints, but solid color is more desirable. Every color supposes the obligatory dark lips and eye rims. Widespread solid piebald color and speckling on the muzzle and legs are not desirable.

Height: Height at withers: for males not lower than 68 cm; for females not lower than 64 cm. The desirable height for males is 72–75 cm, for females 66–69 cm.
  Faults: Height in withers for males lower than 65 cm; for females lower than 62 cm.

Disqualifying Faults:
• Coward, choleric, uncontrolled aggressiveness.
• A dog with a feminine type.

• All deviations from the standard bite; lack of any tooth.
• An inborn bobbed tail.
• Soft, wavy, very short (moleskin) hair.
• All variants of black color (except a black mask), all variants of liver color or all variants of blue color. Genetically weak pigment: ash combined with the gray eye rims and light eyes; fawn or light red combined with brown lips and eye rims, a brown nose and light eyes.
• Bi- or unilateral cryptorchidism.

BETTER THAN THE AVERAGE DOG

Even though you may never show your dog, you should still read the breed standard. The breed standard tells you more than just physical specifications such as how tall your dog should be; it also describes how he should act, how he should move and what unique qualities make him the breed that he is. You are not investing money in a pure-bred dog so that you can own a dog that "sort of looks like" the breed you're purchasing. You want a typical, handsome representative of the breed, one that all of your friends and family and people you meet out in public will recognize as the breed you've so carefully selected and researched. If the parents of your prospective puppy bear little or no resemblance to the dog described in the breed standard, you should keep searching!

Here's a beautiful short-coated Caucasian. The head should be wide and solid, with dark eyes, a black nose (in most colors) and ears cropped close to the head.

CAUCASIAN MOUNTAIN DOG

HOW TO SELECT A CAUCASIAN PUPPY

You can't pick your human relatives, but you can choose your new canine family member. You should pick your Caucasian Mountain Dog puppy very carefully because breed ownership is at least a decade-long commitment. Familiarize yourself with the Caucasian Mountain Dog breed standard and especially the temperament characteristics of the breed prior to looking for a puppy. By reading and studying the breed's traits, it should be quite clear to you that this is not a breed for everyone. A wonderful place to research the breed online is www.caucasiandogs.com, an informational site that links breed fanciers from around the world.

Next, choose a good breeder. While membership in a breed club does not automatically confer respectability, most responsible breeders belong to their regional or national Caucasian club. The Caucasian Ovcharka (Mountain Dog) Club of America can be found online at www.cocaclub.us. Breed clubs usually bind members by a

Drako Faraon Esquire, a bouncing baby boy of seven weeks old, bred and owned by the author.

code of ethics that outlines proper care and treatment of dogs, and sets up a guideline for the relationship between seller and buyer. Ask to see a copy of the code of ethics.

Ask the breeder why he bred this particular litter. Ethical breeders breed only to preserve and improve the breed. Ask the breeder to explain how the litter is expected to contribute to the gene pool and to describe the type of adult dogs that the pups are expected to become. Good breeders typically breed to keep puppies from their own litters, not solely for pet production. Ask what kind of

guarantee the breeder will provide and which situations it covers. Buy from breeders who provide a veterinary health certificate with the puppy sale. Get in writing that you can return the dog within 72 hours if there is a health problem. Then take the pup to a vet for a health check-up before making the final decision.

Good breeders can demonstrate how their breeding stock meets the requirements of the standard, usually by judges' evaluations. Ask to see copies of health screenings and temperament test certificates on the sire and dam, along with any conformation or performance certificates. At a minimum, the sire and dam should be evaluated for hip dysplasia, to help control the expression of this disease in the Caucasian Mountain Dog breed.

Good breeders may breed their bitches to a suitable male in a different city or across the country, but the dam of the litter should always be available for the prospective buyer to meet. The buyer should ask himself if the dam is the kind of dog he wants for his home. An answer of "yes" increases the chances of finding a suitable puppy in the litter.

The litter should be in clean surroundings and all puppies in the litter should appear healthy. The pups should feel firm, rounded and well-fed, but a pot-bellied stomach may indicate

A SHOW PUPPY

If you plan to show your puppy, you must first deal with a reputable breeder who shows his dogs and has had some success in the conformation ring. The puppy's pedigree should include one or more champions in the first and second generation. You should be familiar with the breed and breed standard so you can know what qualities to look for in your puppy. The breeder's observations and recommendations also are invaluable aids in selecting your future champion. If you consider an older puppy, be sure that the puppy has been properly socialized with people, animals and situations, not isolated in a kennel, as early socialization is so essential in this breed.

Six weeks old and on the prowl is Jette Esquire, a female Caucasian pup bred and owned by the author.

worms. Pick up a pinch of skin on the back and release it. The flesh should return to its original shape if the pup is not dehydrated. There should be no discharge from any puppy's nose or eyes. Lift the tail and check for diarrhea residue. The skin should not have dandruff or look dry. The puppy should stand on strong legs and good feet. Open the puppy's mouth and observe if the teeth meet well.

Choose a puppy that appears happy and outgoing, not shy or fearful. Ask the breeder for recommendations on which puppy has the most suitable personality for your situation, whether you are seeking a Caucasian as a home companion and guard, a show dog, a working dog or a performance dog. Some breeders may choose a puppy for the buyer. Puppies that appear to play very hard or be very aggressive may become problematic adults. A puppy that allows himself to be picked up, turned over and cradled like a baby probably has been handled a lot since birth. This pup should make a nice, well-socialized pet.

All correctly bred Caucasian Mountain Dog puppies look like cute little bear cubs. The best examples of the standard will have huge, almost oversized, wedge-shaped heads with full skulls and deep, short, heavy muzzles without snipiness or foxy appearance. The eyes should be medium in size and oblique, without being overly rounded or having red sclera showing. The body should appear compact and substantial with a wide chest, and the puppy should feel dense and heavy to pick up. The legs should have huge bone with large, rounded, compact feet. "Pet-qual-

GETTING ACQUAINTED
When visiting a litter, ask the breeder for suggestions on how best to interact with the puppies. If possible, get right into the middle of the pack and sit down with them. Observe which pups climb into your lap and which ones shy away. Toss a toy for them to chase and bring back to you. It's easy to fall in love with the puppy who picks you, but keep your future objectives in mind before you make your final decision.

ity" puppies may deviate from the ideal description but they should still show strong breed characteristics and be as healthy and sound as all of the other puppies. Nine to twelve weeks of age is a good time for a puppy to leave the litter. The breeder should supply the registration paperwork as well as records of vaccination and worming.

A COMMITTED NEW OWNER
By now you should understand what makes the Caucasian Mountain Dog a most unique and special dog, one that you've determined may fit nicely into your family and lifestyle. If you have researched breeders, you should be able to recognize a knowledgeable and responsible Caucasian Mountain Dog breeder who cares not only about his pups but also about what kind of owner you will be. If you have completed the final step in your new journey, you have found a litter, or possibly two, of quality Caucasian Mountain Dog pups.

A visit with the puppies and their breeder should be an education in itself. Breed research, breeder selection and puppy visitation are very important aspects of finding the puppy of your dreams. Beyond that, these things also lay the foundation for a successful future with your pup. Puppy personalities within each litter vary, from the shy and easygoing puppy to the one who is dominant

> **SIGNS OF A HEALTHY PUPPY**
> Healthy puppies are robust little fellows who are alert and active, sporting shiny coats and supple skin. They should not appear lethargic, bloated or pot-bellied, nor should they have flaky skin or runny or crusted eyes or noses. Their stools should be firm and well formed, with no evidence of blood or mucus.

and assertive, with most pups falling somewhere in between. By spending time with the puppies, you will be able to recognize certain behaviors and what these behaviors indicate about each pup's temperament.

Which type of pup will complement your family dynamics is best determined by observing the puppies in action within their "pack." Your breeder's expertise and recommendations are also valuable. Although you may fall in love with a bold and brassy male, the breeder may suggest that another pup would be best for you. The breeder's experience in rearing Caucasian Mountain Dog pups and matching their temperaments with appropriate humans offers the best assurance that your pup will meet your needs and expectations. The type of puppy that you select is just as important as your decision that the Caucasian Mountain Dog is the breed for you.

The decision to live with a Caucasian Mountain Dog is a seri-

CREATE A SCHEDULE

Puppies thrive on sameness and routine. Offer meals at the same time each day, take him out at regular times for potty trips and do the same for play periods and outdoor activity. Make note of when your puppy naps and when he is most lively and energetic, and try to plan his day around those times. Once he is house-trained and more predictable in his habits, he will be better able to tolerate changes in his schedule.

the basics of survival—food, water, shelter and protection—he needs much, much more. The new pup needs love, nurturing, socialization and a proper canine education to mold him into a responsible, well-behaved canine citizen. Your Caucasian's health and good manners will need consistent monitoring and regular "tune-ups," so your job as a responsible dog owner will be ongoing throughout every stage of his life. If you are not prepared to accept these responsibilities and commit to them for the next decade, likely longer, then you are not prepared to own a dog of any breed.

Although the responsibilities of owning a dog may at times tax your patience, the joy of living with your Caucasian Mountain Dog far outweighs the workload, and a well-mannered adult dog is worth your time and effort. Before your very eyes, your new charge will grow up to be your most loyal friend, devoted to you unconditionally.

YOUR CAUCASIAN MOUNTAIN DOG SHOPPING LIST

Just as expectant parents prepare a nursery for their baby, so should you ready your home for the arrival of your Caucasian Mountain Dog pup. If you have the necessary puppy supplies purchased and in place before he comes home, it will ease the puppy's transition from the

ous commitment and not one to be taken lightly. This puppy is a living sentient being that will be dependent on you for basic survival for his entire life. Beyond warmth and familiarity of his mom and littermates to the brand-new environment of his new home and human family. You will be too busy to stock up and prepare your house after your pup comes home, that's for sure! Imagine how a puppy must feel upon being transported to a strange new place. It's up to you to comfort him and to let your little pup know that he is going to be happy with you.

FOOD AND WATER BOWLS

Your puppy will need separate bowls for his food and water. Stainless steel pans are generally preferred over plastic bowls since they sterilize better and pups are less inclined to chew on the metal. Heavy-duty ceramic bowls are popular, but consider how often you will have to pick up those heavy bowls. Buy adult-sized pans, as your puppy will grow into them before you know it.

THE DOG CRATE

If you think that crates are tools of punishment and confinement for when a dog has misbehaved, think again. Most breeders and almost all trainers recommend a crate as the preferred house-training aid as well as for all-around puppy training and safety. Because dogs are natural den creatures that prefer cave-like environments, the benefits of crate use are many. The crate

THE FAMILY TREE
Your puppy's pedigree is his family tree. Just as a child may resemble his parents and grandparents, so too will a puppy reflect the qualities, good and bad, of his ancestors, especially those in the first two generations. Therefore, it's important to know as much as possible about a puppy's immediate relatives. Reputable and experienced breeders should be able to explain the pedigree and why they chose to breed from the particular dogs they used.

provides the puppy with his very own "safe house," a cozy place to sleep, take a break or seek comfort with a favorite toy; a travel aid to house your dog when on the road, at motels or at the vet's office; a training aid to help teach your puppy proper

The three most common crate types: mesh on the left, wire on the right and fiberglass on top.

toileting habits; a place of solitude where your puppy or adult dog can rest when non-dog people happen to drop by.

Crates come in several types, although the wire crate and the fiberglass airline-type crate are the most popular. Both are safe and your puppy will adjust to either one, so the choice is up to you. The wire crates offer better visibility for the pup as well as better ventilation. Many of the wire crates fold down for easy transport. The fiberglass crates, similar to those used by the airlines for animal transport, are sturdier and more den-like. However, the fiberglass crates do not collapse and are less ventilated than a wire crate, which can be problematic in hot weather. Some of the newer crates are made of heavy plastic mesh; they are very lightweight and fold up into slim-line suitcases. However, a mesh crate might not

be suitable for a pup with manic chewing habits and is not suitable for a powerful Caucasian adult.

Wire crates are good for use in the home. Fiberglass crates are usually the crates of choice for traveling, although both types can double as travel crates, providing protection for the dog. The size of the crate is another thing to consider. Bigger is better when it comes to your new Russian giant! You want to purchase a crate that will accommodate your Caucasian at his full size. For a male, you will want to purchase the giant size (45" high by 37" wide by 54" deep) and for a female, the extra-large size (at least 36" high by 30" wide by 48" deep). For house-training purposes, you can use a removable divider panel to initially create a smaller space for the pup.

BEDDING AND CRATE PADS
Your puppy will enjoy some type of soft bedding in his "room" (the crate), something he can snuggle into to feel cozy and secure. Old towels or blankets are good choices for a young pup, since he may (and probably will) have a toileting accident or two in the crate or decide to chew on the bedding material. Once he is fully trained and out of the early chewing stage, you can replace the puppy bedding with a permanent crate pad if you prefer. Crate pads and other dog beds run the gamut

from inexpensive to high-end doggie-designer styles, but don't splurge on the good stuff until you are sure that your puppy is reliable and won't tear it up or make a mess on it.

PUPPY TOYS

Just as infants and older children require objects to stimulate their minds and bodies, puppies need toys to entertain their curious brains, wiggly paws and achy teeth. A fun array of safe doggie toys will help satisfy your puppy's chewing instincts and distract him from gnawing on the leg of your antique chair or your new leather sofa. Most puppy toys are cute and look as if they would be a lot of fun, but not all are necessarily safe or good for your puppy, so use caution when you go puppy-toy shopping.

Adult Caucasian Mountain Dogs are not especially aggressive chewers, but puppies are very large with strong jaws that can damage shoes and furniture. The best "chewcifiers" are nylon and hard rubber bones, which are safe to gnaw on and come in sizes appropriate for all age groups and breeds. Raw (never cooked) marrow and knuckle bones will occupy both pups and adults for hours, but be careful of natural bones, which can splinter or develop dangerous sharp edges. Dogs can easily swallow or choke on those bone splinters. Veterinari-

TOYS 'R SAFE

The vast array of tantalizing puppy toys is staggering. Stroll through any pet shop or pet-supply outlet and you will see that the choices can be overwhelming. However, not all dog toys are safe or sensible. Most very young puppies enjoy soft woolly toys that they can snuggle with and carry around. (You know they have outgrown them when they shred them up!) Avoid toys that have buttons, tabs or other enhancements that can be chewed off and swallowed. Soft toys that squeak are fun, but make sure your puppy does not disembowel the toy and remove (and swallow) the squeaker. Toys that rattle or make noise can excite a puppy, but they present the same danger as the squeaky kind and so require supervision. Hard rubber toys that bounce can also entertain a pup, but make sure that the toy is too big for your pup to swallow.

This plastic hamburger toy won't last much longer than the real thing! Only offer squeaky toys under supervision and remove them at the first sign of being damaged.

ans often tell of surgical night-mares involving bits of splintered bone, because in addition to the danger of choking, the sharp pieces can damage the intestinal tract.

Similarly, rawhide chews, while a favorite of most dogs and puppies, can be equally dangerous. Pieces of rawhide are easily swallowed after they get soft and gummy from chewing, and dogs have been known to choke on large pieces of ingested rawhide. Rawhide chews should be offered only when you can supervise the puppy.

Soft woolly toys are special puppy favorites. They come in a wide variety of cute shapes and sizes; some look like little stuffed animals. Puppies love to shake them up and toss them about, or simply carry them around. While fun, these toys are destroyed by teething pups in short order. Be careful of fuzzy toys that have button eyes or noses that your pup could chew off and swallow, and

Your Caucasian pup will likely make his own chew toys, so keep a close eye on the "souvenirs" he picks up on his trips around the yard.

make sure that he does not disembowel a squeaky toy to remove the squeaker! Braided rope toys are similar in that they are fun to chew and toss around, but they shred easily and the strings are easy to swallow. The strings are not digestible and, if the puppy does not pass them in his stool, he could end up at the vet's office. As with rawhides, your puppy should be closely monitored with soft, squeaky and rope toys.

If you believe that your pup has ingested a piece of one of his toys, check his stools for the next couple of days to see if he passes the item when he defecates. At the same time, also watch for signs of intestinal distress. A call to your veterinarian might be in order to get his advice and be on the safe side.

An all-time favorite toy for puppies (young and old!) is the empty gallon milk jug. Hard plastic juice containers—46 ounces or more—are also excellent. Such containers make lots of noise when

they are batted about, and puppies go crazy with delight as they play with them. However, they likely won't last more than a few minutes, so be sure to remove them right away when they get chewed up.

The best thing to do is to supervise your Caucasian Mountain Dog when he's playing with any potentially destructible toys, and offer him safe sturdy chews, such as large nylon bones, for free play. Monitor the condition of all of your pup's toys carefully and get rid of any that have been chewed to the point of becoming potentially dangerous.

A word of caution about homemade toys: be careful with your choices of non-traditional

play objects. Never use old shoes or socks, since a puppy cannot distinguish between the old ones on which he's allowed to chew and the new ones in your closet that are strictly off-limits. That principle applies to anything that resembles something that you don't want your puppy to chew.

Puppies are naturally curious and your Caucasian will be no different—snooping around and sticking his nose into whatever he can find!

TEETHING TIME

All puppies chew. It's normal canine behavior. Chewing just plain feels good to a puppy, especially during the three- to five-month teething period when the adult teeth are breaking through the gums. Rather than attempting to eliminate such a strong natural chewing instinct, you will be more successful if you redirect it and teach your puppy what he may or may not chew. Correct inappropriate chewing with a sharp "No!" and offer him a chew toy, praising him when he takes it. Don't become discouraged. Chewing usually decreases after the adult teeth have come in.

COLLARS

A lightweight nylon collar is the best choice for a very young pup. Quick-clip collars are easy to put on and remove, and they can be adjusted as the puppy grows. Introduce him to his collar as soon as he comes home to get him accustomed to wearing it. He'll get used to it quickly and won't mind a bit. Make sure that it is snug enough that it won't slip off, yet loose enough to be comfortable for the pup. Keep in mind that the Caucasian Mountain Dog has quite a bit of hair growing around his neck. You should be able to slip two

COLLARING OUR CANINES

The standard flat collar with a buckle or a snap, in leather, nylon or cotton, is widely regarded as the everyday all-purpose collar. If the collar fits correctly, you should be able to fit two fingers between the collar and the dog's neck.

Leather Buckle Collars

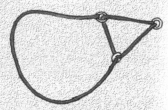

Limited-Slip Collar

The martingale, Greyhound or limited-slip collar is preferred by many dog owners and trainers. It is fixed with an extra loop that tightens when pressure is applied to the leash. The martingale collar gets tighter but does not "choke" the dog. The limited-slip collar should only be used for walking and training, not for free play or interaction with another dog. These types of collar should never be left on the dog, as the extra loop can lead to accidents.

Chain choke collars, usually made of stainless steel, are made for training purposes, though are not recommended for small dogs or heavily coated breeds. The chains can injure small dogs or damage long/abundant coats. Thin nylon choke leads are commonly used on show dogs while in the ring, though they are not practical for everyday use.

The harness, with two or three straps that attach over the dog's shoulders and around his torso, is a humane and safe alternative to the conventional collar. By and large, a well-made harness is virtually escape-proof. Harnesses are available in nylon and mesh and can be outfitted on most dogs, with chest girths ranging from 10 to 30 inches.

Snap Bolt Choke Collar

Harness

Nylon Collar

Quick-Click Closure

Snake Chain

Chrome Steel

Fur-Saver

Choke Chain Collars

A head collar, composed of a nylon strap that goes around the dog's muzzle and a second strap that wraps around his neck, offers the owner better control over his dog. This device is recommended for problem-solving with dogs (including jumping up, pulling and aggressive behaviors), but must be used with care.

A training halter, including a flat collar and two straps, made of nylon and webbing, is designed for walking. There are several on the market; some are more difficult to put on the dog than others. The halter harness, with two small slip rings at each end, is recommended for ease of use.

CONFINEMENT

It is wise to keep your puppy confined to a small "puppy-proofed" area of the house for his first few weeks at home. Gate or block off a space near the door he will use for outdoor potty trips. Expandable baby gates are useful to create puppy's designated area. If he is allowed to roam through the entire house or even only several rooms, it will be more difficult to house-train him.

fingers between the collar and his neck. Check the collar often, as puppies grow in spurts, and his collar can become too tight almost overnight. Choke collars are for training purposes only and should never be used on a puppy. With a grown Caucasian, choke collars must be removed right away after training and do not use a chain choke, as this will damage the neck fur.

LEASHES

A 6-foot nylon lead is an excellent choice for a young puppy. It is lightweight and not as tempting to chew as a leather lead. You can switch to a 6-foot leather lead after your pup has grown and is used to walking politely on a lead. For initial puppy walks and house-training purposes, you should invest in a shorter lead so that you have more control over the puppy. At first you don't want him wandering too far away from

you, and when taking him out for toileting you will want to keep him in the specific area chosen for his potty spot.

HOME SAFETY FOR YOUR PUPPY

The importance of puppy-proofing cannot be overstated. In addition to making your house comfortable for your Caucasian's arrival, you also must make sure that your house is safe for your puppy before you bring him home. There are countless hazards in the owner's personal living environment that a pup can sniff, chew, swallow or destroy. Many are obvious; others are not. Do a thorough advance house check to remove or rearrange those things that could hurt your puppy, keeping any potentially dangerous items out of areas to which he will have access.

Electrical cords are especially dangerous, since puppies view them as irresistible chow toys. Unplug and remove all exposed

A weak spot in a fence is no match for a Caucasian pup who wants to see what's on the other side. Keep this in mind when puppy-proofing the outdoor areas to which your pup will have access.

A Dog-Safe Home

The dog-safety police are taking you and your new puppy on a house tour. Let's go room by room and see how safe your own home is for your new pup. The following items are doggie dangers for dogs of all ages, so either they must be removed or the dog should be monitored or not have access to these areas.

LIVING ROOM
- house plants (some varieties are poisonous)
- fireplace or wood-burning stove
- paint on the walls (lead-based paint is toxic)
- lead drapery weights (toxic lead)
- lamps and electrical cords
- carpet cleaners or deodorizers

OUTDOOR
- swimming pool
- pesticides
- toxic plants
- lawn fertilizers

BATHROOM
- blue water in the toilet bowl
- medicine cabinet (filled with potentially deadly bottles)
- soap bars, bleach, drain cleaners, etc.
- tampons

KITCHEN
- household cleaners in the kitchen cabinets
- glass jars and canisters
- sharp objects (like kitchen knives, scissors and forks)
- garbage can (with remnants of good-smelling things like onions, potato skins, apple or pear cores, peach pits, coffee beans, etc.)
- "people foods" that are toxic to dogs, like chocolate, raisins, grapes, nuts and onions

GARAGE
- antifreeze
- fertilizers (including rose foods)
- pesticides and rodenticides
- pool supplies (chlorine and other chemicals)
- oil and gasoline in containers
- sharp objects, electrical cords and power tools

cords or fasten them beneath a baseboard where the puppy cannot reach them. Veterinarians and firefighters can tell you horror stories about electrical burns and house fires that resulted from puppy-chewed electrical cords. Consider this a most serious precaution for your puppy and the rest of your family.

Scout your home for tiny objects that might be seen at a pup's eye level. Keep medication bottles and cleaning supplies well out of reach, and do the same with wastebaskets and other trash containers. It goes without saying that you should not use rodent poison or other toxic chemicals in any puppy area and that you must keep such containers safely locked up. You will be amazed at how many places a curious puppy can discover!

Once your house has cleared inspection, check your yard. Caucasian Mountain Dogs tend not to be jumpers, though there are exceptions. They will go through fences when protecting property by climbing or digging out. The fence must be well embedded into the ground and high enough so that it really is impossible for your dog to get over it. A minimum of 6-foot-high fencing is recommended along with hotwire as needed. Reinforce latches so that they can't be batted or nudged open by a persistent paw or nose, as a Caucasian can

figure out how to open a latch. Be sure to repair or secure any gaps in the fence, and check the fence periodically to ensure that it is in good shape. A very determined (or very bored) pup may return to the same spot to "work on it" until he is able to get through.

The garage and shed can be hazardous places for a pup, as things like fertilizers, chemicals and tools are usually kept there. It's best to keep these areas off-limits to the pup. Antifreeze is especially dangerous to dogs, as they find the taste appealing and it takes only a few licks from the driveway to kill a dog, puppy or adult, small breed or large.

Future water dog? Not all dogs take to water, but if your pup wants to give it a try, introduce swimming lessons slowly and in a safe setting.

VISITING THE VETERINARIAN
A good veterinarian is your Caucasian puppy's best health-insurance policy. If you do not already have a vet, ask friends and experienced dog people in your area for recommendations so that you can select a vet with experience in large-breed dogs before

> ### PUPPY PARASITES
> Parasites are nasty little critters that live in or on your dog or puppy. Most puppies are born with ascarid roundworms, which are acquired from dormant ascarids residing in the dam. Other parasites can be acquired through contact with infected fecal matter. Take a stool sample to your vet for testing. He will prescribe a safe wormer to treat any parasites found in your puppy's stool. Always have a fecal test performed at your puppy's annual veterinary exam.

ing a health journal for your puppy will make a handy reference for his wellness and any future health problems that may arise.

MEETING THE FAMILY

Your Caucasian Mountain Dog's homecoming is an exciting time for all members of the family, and it's only natural that everyone will be eager to meet him, pet him and play with him. However, for the puppy's sake, it's best to make these initial family meetings as uneventful as possible so that the pup is not overwhelmed with too much too soon. Remember, he has just left his dam and his littermates and is away from the breeder's home for the first time. Despite his fuzzy wagging tail, he is still apprehensive and wondering where he is and who

you bring your Caucasian puppy home. Also arrange for your puppy's first veterinary examination beforehand, since many vets have two- and three-week waiting periods and your puppy should visit the vet within a day or so of coming home.

His littermates and breeder have always been there to give him a lift! Your pup will miss those familiar faces when he first comes home with you.

It's important to make sure your puppy's first visit to the vet is a pleasant and positive one. The vet should take great care to befriend the pup and handle him gently to make their first meeting a positive experience. The vet will give the pup a thorough physical examination and set up a schedule for vaccinations and other necessary wellness visits. Be sure to show your vet any health and inoculation records, which you should have received from your breeder. Your vet is a great source of canine health information, so be sure to ask questions and take notes. Creat-

all these strange humans are. It's best to let him explore on his own and meet the family members as he feels comfortable. Let him investigate all the new smells, sights and sounds at his own pace. Children should be especially careful to not get overly excited, use loud voices or hug the pup too tightly. Be calm, gentle and affectionate, and be ready to comfort him if he appears frightened or uneasy.

Be sure to show your puppy his new crate during this first day home. Toss a treat or two inside the crate; if he associates the crate with food, he will associate the crate with good things. If he is comfortable with the crate, you can offer him his first meal inside it. Leave the door ajar so he can wander in and out as he chooses.

FIRST NIGHT IN HIS NEW HOME
So much has happened in your Caucasian Mountain Dog puppy's first day away from the breeder. He's had his first car ride to his new home. He's met his new human family and perhaps the other family pets. He has explored his new house and yard, at least those places where he is to be allowed during his first weeks at home. He may have visited his new veterinarian. He has eaten his first meal or two away from his dam and littermates. Surely that's enough to tire out a ten-week-old

SELECTING FROM THE LITTER
Before you visit a litter of puppies, promise yourself that you won't fall for the first pretty face you see! Decide on your goals for your puppy—show prospect, guard dog, obedience competitor, family companion—and then look for a puppy who displays the appropriate qualities. In most litters, there is an alpha pup (the bossy puppy), and occasionally a shy fellow who is less confident, with the rest of the litter falling somewhere in the middle. "Middle-of-the-roaders" are safe bets for most families and novice competitors.

Caucasian Mountain Dog pup...or so you hope!

It's bedtime. During the day, the pup investigated his crate, which is his new den and sleeping space, so it is not entirely strange to him. Line the crate with a soft towel or blanket that he can snuggle into and gently place him into the crate for the night. Some breeders send home a piece of

Attention, affection and gentle handling will help your Caucasian pup make the transition from the puppy pack to his new pack, you and your family.

puppy will learn that crying means "out" and will continue that habit. You are laying the groundwork for future habits. Some breeders find that soft music can soothe a crying pup and help him get to sleep.

bedding from where the pup slept with his littermates, and those familiar scents are a great comfort for the puppy on his first night without his siblings.

He will probably whine or cry. The puppy is objecting to the confinement and the fact that he is alone for the first time. This can be a stressful time for you as well as for the pup. It's important that you remain strong and don't let the puppy out of his crate to comfort him. He will fall asleep eventually. If you release him, the

SOCIALIZING YOUR PUPPY

The first 20 weeks of your Caucasian Mountain Dog puppy's life are the most important of his entire lifetime. A properly socialized puppy will grow up to be a confident and stable adult dog who will be a pleasure to live with and a welcome addition to the neighborhood.

The importance of socialization cannot be overemphasized. Research on canine behavior has proven that puppies who are not exposed to new sights, sounds, people and animals during their first 20 weeks of life will grow up to be timid and fearful, even aggressive, and unable to flourish outside of their familiar home environment.

Happy puppies come running, and this is a veritable Caucasian stampede!

Socializing your puppy is not difficult and, in fact, will be a fun time for you both. Lead training goes hand in hand with socialization, so your puppy will be learning how to walk on a lead at the same time that he's meeting the neighborhood. Because the Caucasian Mountain Dog is such a fascinating breed, people will enjoy meeting "the new ovcharka on the block." Take him for short walks, to the park and to other dog-friendly places where he will encounter new people, especially children. Caucasians are naturally suspicious of strangers—keep this in mind—your dog will never be a tail-wagging Golden Retriever, but he still must be biddable around strangers. Just make sure that you supervise these meetings and that the children do not get too rough or encourage him to play too hard. A bad experience in puppyhood can impact a dog for life, so a pup that has a negative experience with a child may grow up to be shy or even aggressive around children.

Take your puppy along on your daily errands. Puppies are natural "people magnets," and most people who see your pup will want to pet him. All of these encounters will help to mold him into a confident adult dog. Likewise, you will soon feel like a confident, responsible dog owner, rightly proud of your handsome

and, most importantly, well-behaved Caucasian Mountain Dog.

Be especially careful of your puppy's encounters and experiences during the eight-to-ten-week-old period, if you have him during this time; this is also called the "fear period." This is a serious imprinting period, and all contact during this time should be gentle and positive. A frightening or negative event could leave a permanent impression that could affect his future behavior if a similar situation arises. This can manifest itself in fear and aggression as the dog grows up; shyness and

Make sure to supervise your Caucasian's interaction with strange children.

A Russian bear cub with an itch!

NEW RELEASES

Most Caucasian Mountain Dog breeders release their puppies between 9 and 12 weeks of age. A breeder who allows puppies to leave the litter earlier may be more concerned with profit than with the puppies' welfare. However, some breeders of show or working breeds may hold one or more top-quality puppies longer, occasionally until three or four months of age, in order to evaluate the puppies' career or show potential and decide which one(s) they will keep for themselves.

over-wariness of strangers also can be problems in the Caucasian Mountain Dog that has not been properly socialized. Your puppy needs lots of positive interaction, which of course includes human contact, affection, handling and exposure to other animals.

Also make sure that your puppy has received his first and second rounds of vaccinations before you expose him to other dogs or bring him to places that other dogs may frequent. Avoid dog parks and other strange-dog areas until your vet assures you that your puppy is fully immunized and resistant to the diseases that can be passed between canines. Discuss socialization with your breeder, as some breeders recommend socializing the puppy even before he has received all of his inoculations, depending on how outgoing the puppy may be.

LEADER OF THE PUPPY'S PACK

The Caucasian, being a naturally pack-oriented canine, needs an authority figure, someone he can look up to and regard as the leader of his "pack." His first pack leader was his dam, who taught him to be polite and not chew too hard on her ears or nip at her muzzle. He learned those same lessons from his littermates. If he played too rough, they cried in pain and stopped the game, which sent an important message to the rowdy puppy.

As puppies play together, they are also struggling to determine who will be the boss. Again, being pack animals, dogs need someone to be in charge. If a litter of puppies remained together beyond puppyhood, one of the pups would emerge as the strongest one, the one who calls the shots.

Once your puppy leaves the pack, he will look intuitively for a new leader. If he does not recognize you as that leader, he will try to assume that position for himself. Don't let your Caucasian pup's small size and youth fool you when it comes to his positioning for a place in the pack. You must remember that these are natural canine instincts. Do not cave in and allow your pup to get the upper "paw"!

Just as socialization is so important during these first 20 weeks, so too is your puppy's early

education. He was born without any bad habits. He does not know what is good or bad behavior. If he does things like nipping and digging, it's because he is having fun and doesn't know that humans consider these things as "bad." It's your job to teach him proper puppy manners, and this is the best time to accomplish that... before he has developed bad habits, since it is much more difficult to "unlearn" or correct unacceptable learned behavior than to teach good behavior from the start.

Make sure that all members of the family understand the importance of being consistent when training their new puppy. If you tell the puppy to stay off the sofa and your daughter allows him to cuddle on the couch with her to watch her favorite TV show, your pup will be confused about what he is and is not allowed to do. Have a family conference before your pup comes home so that everyone understands the basic principles of puppy training and

A well-socialized Caucasian should be amenable to all types of handling from his owner. These ministrations should start in puppyhood to encourage a well-adjusted adult who will not struggle with routine grooming and examination.

FINDING A QUALIFIED BREEDER

Before you begin your puppy search, ask for references from your veterinarian and perhaps other breeders to refer you to someone they believe is reputable. Responsible breeders usually raise only one or two breeds of dog. Avoid any breeder who has several different breeds or has several litters at the same time. Dedicated breeders are usually involved with a breed or other dog club. Many participate in some sport or activity related to their breed. Just as you want to be assured of the breeder's qualifications, the breeder wants to be assured that you will make a worthy owner. Expect the breeder to interview you, asking questions about your goals for the pup, your experience with dogs and what kind of home you will provide.

Belly up! On his back with stomach exposed is a submissive posture, showing that the pup is comfortable with you and trusts you as his leader (and groomer!).

by tossing a toy for him to fetch. You also will be able to whisk him outside when you notice that he is about to piddle on the carpet. If you can't see your puppy, you can't teach him or correct his behavior.

SOLVING PUPPY PROBLEMS

CHEWING AND NIPPING

Nipping at fingers and toes is normal puppy behavior. Chewing is also the way that puppies investigate their surroundings. However, you will have to teach your puppy that chewing anything other than his toys is not acceptable. That won't happen overnight and at times puppy teeth will test your patience. However, if you allow nipping and chewing to continue, just think about the damage that a mature Caucasian Mountain Dog can do with a full set of adult teeth.

Whenever your puppy nips your hand or fingers, cry out

the rules you have set forth for the pup, and agrees to follow them.

The old adage that "an ounce of prevention is worth a pound of cure" is especially true when it comes to puppies. It is much easier to prevent inappropriate behavior than it is to change it. It's also easier and less stressful for the pup, since it will keep discipline to a minimum and create a more positive learning environment for him. That, in turn, will also be easier on you.

Here are a few commonsense tips to keep your belongings safe and your puppy out of trouble:
- Keep your closet doors closed and your shoes, socks and other apparel off the floor so your puppy can't get at them.
- Keep a secure lid on the trash container or put the trash where your puppy can't dig into it. He can't eat what he can't reach!
- Supervise your puppy at all times to make sure he is not getting into mischief. If he starts to chew the corner of the rug, you can distract him instantly

TOXIC PLANTS

Plants are natural puppy magnets, but many can be harmful, even fatal, if ingested by a puppy or adult dog. Scout your yard and home interior and remove any plants, bushes or flowers that could be even mildly dangerous. It could save your puppy's life. You can obtain a complete list of toxic plants from your veterinarian, at the public library or by looking online.

"Ouch!" in a loud voice, which should startle your puppy and stop him from nipping, even if only for a moment. Immediately distract him by offering a small treat or an appropriate toy for him to chew instead (which means having chew toys and puppy treats handy or in your pockets at all times). Praise him when he takes the toy and tell him what a good fellow he is. Praise is just as or even more important in puppy training as discipline and correction.

Puppies also tend to nip at children more often than adults, since they perceive little ones to be more vulnerable and more similar to their littermates. Teach your children appropriate responses to nipping behavior. If they are unable to handle it themselves, you may have to intervene. Puppy nips can be quite painful and a child's frightened reaction will only encourage a puppy to nip harder, which is a natural canine response. As with all other puppy situations, interaction between your Caucasian Mountain Dog puppy and children should be supervised.

Chewing on objects, not just family members' fingers and ankles, is also normal canine behavior that can be especially tedious (for the owner, not the pup) during the teething period when the puppy's adult teeth are

REPEAT YOURSELF
Puppies learn best through repetition. Use the same verbal cues and commands when teaching your puppy new behaviors or correcting for misbehaviors. Be consistent, but not monotonous. Puppies get bored just like puppy owners.

coming in. At this stage, chewing just plain feels good. Furniture legs and cabinet corners are common puppy favorites. Shoes and other personal items also taste pretty good to a pup.

The best solution is, once again, prevention. If you value something, keep it tucked away and out of reach. You can't hide your dining-room table in a closet, but you can try to deflect the chewing by applying a bitter product made just to deter dogs from chewing. Available in a spray or cream, this substance is vile-tasting, although safe for dogs, and most puppies will avoid the forbidden object after one tiny taste. You also can apply the product to your leather leash if the puppy tries to chew on his lead during leash-training sessions.

Keep a ready supply of safe chews handy to offer your Caucasian Mountain Dog as a distraction when he starts to chew on something that's a "no-no." Remember, at this tender age he does not yet know what is permitted or forbidden, so you have to be "on call" every minute he's awake and on the prowl.

You may lose a treasure or two during puppy's growing-up period, and the furniture could sustain a nasty nick or two. These can be trying times, so be prepared for those inevitable accidents and comfort yourself in knowing that this too shall pass.

Jumping Up

Puppies jump up...on you, your guests, your counters and your furniture. Just another normal part of growing up, and one you need to meet head-on before it becomes an ingrained habit. This breed is way too big to grow up thinking that jumping up is an acceptable form of greeting.

The key to jump correction is consistency. You cannot correct your Caucasian Mountain Dog for jumping up on you today, then allow it to happen tomorrow by greeting him with hugs and kisses. As you have learned by now, consistency is critical to all puppy lessons.

For starters, try turning your

WATCH THE WATER

To help your puppy sleep through the night without having to relieve himself, remove his water bowl after 7 p.m. Offer him a couple of ice cubes during the evening to quench his thirst. Never leave water in a puppy's crate, as this is inviting puddles of mishaps.

back as soon as the puppy jumps. Jumping up is a means of gaining your attention and, if the pup can't see your face, he may get discouraged and learn that he loses eye contact with his beloved master when he jumps up.

Leash corrections also work, and most puppies respond well to a leash tug if they jump. Grasp the leash close to the puppy's collar and give a quick tug downward, using the command "Off." Do not use the word "Down," since "Down" is used to teach the puppy to lie down, which is a separate action that he will learn during his education in the basic commands. As soon as the puppy has backed off, tell him to sit and immediately praise him for doing so. This will take many repetitions and won't be accomplished quickly, so don't get discouraged or give up; you must be even more persistent than your puppy.

A second method used for jump correction is the spritzer bottle. Fill a spray bottle with water mixed with a bit of lemon juice or vinegar. As soon as puppy jumps, command him "Off" and spritz him with the water mixture. Of course, that means having the spray bottle handy whenever or wherever jumping usually happens.

Yet a third method to discourage jumping is grasping the puppy's paws and holding them gently but firmly until he strug-

TASTY LESSONS

The best route to teaching a very young puppy is through his tummy. Use tiny bits of soft puppy treats to teach obedience commands like come, sit and down. Don't overdo treats: schooltime is not meant to be mealtime.

gles to get away. Wait a brief moment or two, then release his paws and give him a command to sit. He should eventually learn that jumping gets him into an uncomfortable predicament.

Children are major victims of puppy jumping, since puppies view little people as ready targets for jumping up as well as nipping. If your children (or their friends) are unable to dispense jump corrections, you will have to intervene and handle it for them.

Important to prevention is also knowing what you should not do. Never kick your Caucasian Mountain Dog (for any reason, not just for jumping) or knock him in the chest with your knee. That maneuver could actually harm your puppy. Vets can tell you stories about puppies who suffered broken bones after being banged about when they jumped up.

"COUNTER SURFING"

What we like to call "counter surfing" is a normal extension of jumping and usually starts to happen as soon as a puppy realizes that he is big enough to stand on his hind legs and investigate the good stuff on the kitchen counter or the coffee table. Once again, you have to be there to prevent it! As soon as you see your Caucasian Mountain Dog even start to raise himself up, startle him with a sharp "No!" or "Aaahh, aaahh!" If he succeeds and manages to get one or both paws on the forbidden surface, toll him "Off!" as you remove his paws from the surface and place them on the floor. As soon as he's back on all four paws, command him to sit and praise at once.

For surf prevention, make sure to keep any tempting treats or edibles out of reach, where your Caucasian Mountain Dog can't see or smell them. It's the old rule of prevention yet again.

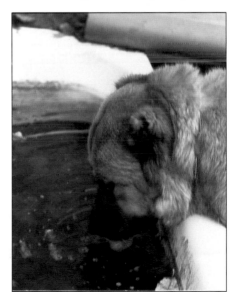

This is not what we mean by providing plenty of water, but the Caucasian Mountain Dog is certainly tall enough to sip from the hot tub! Caucasian owners have to be creative in keeping things out of their dogs' reach.

CAUCASIAN MOUNTAIN DOG

FEEDING CONSIDERATIONS

The Caucasian Mountain Dog is a very "easy keeper" that does well on a quality commercial diet of moderate protein level (about 25%). Adult females will generally consume about 4 cups of kibble per day and adult males 4–6 cups of kibble per day. Kibble can be supplemented with quality canned food, yogurt or home-prepared fresh foods as approved by a veterinarian. Omega-3 supplementation such as a tablespoon of fresh flaxseed can be beneficial.

Every breeder of every dog, regardless of breed, has his own particular way of feeding. Most breeders give the new owner a written record that details the amount and kind of food that the puppy has been receiving, along with recommendations about how to continue feeding as the puppy grows up. Do follow these recommendations to the letter at least for the first month or two after the puppy comes to live with you. Following the prescribed procedure will reduce the chance of upset stomach and loose stools.

Along with indicating the type and amount of food, the diet sheet should indicate the number of times per day that your puppy has been accustomed to being fed and the kind of vitamin supplementation, if any, that he has been receiving. Usually a breeder's diet sheet projects the increases and changes in food that will be necessary as your puppy grows from week to week. If the sheet does not include this information, ask the breeder for suggestions regarding increases and eventual changes to the diet.

If you do your best not to change the puppy's diet when you first bring him home, you will be less likely to run into digestive problems and diarrhea. Diarrhea is very serious in young puppies. Puppies with diarrhea can dehydrate very rapidly, causing severe problems and even death.

If it is necessary to change your Caucasian Mountain Dog puppy's diet for any reason, it should be done gradually, over a period of a few days. Begin by mixing a spoonful or two of the new food in with the old food, gradually increasing the ratio of new food to old food until the meal consists entirely of the new product.

In order for a canine diet to qualify as "complete and balanced" in the United States, it must meet standards set by the Subcommittee on Canine Nutrition of the National Research Council of the National Academy of Sciences. Most commercial foods manufactured for dogs meet

Feeding a Caucasian pup means providing complete nutrition for healthy growth at an even pace.

SWITCHING FOODS

There are certain times in a dog's life when it becomes necessary to switch his food; for example, from puppy to adult food and then from adult to senior-dog food. Additionally, you may decide to feed your pup a different type of food from what he received from the breeder, and there may be "emergency" situations in which you can't find your dog's normal brand and have to offer something else temporarily. Anytime a change is made, for whatever reason, the switch must be done gradually. You don't want to upset the dog's stomach or end up with a picky eater who refuses to eat something new. A tried-and-true approach is, over the course of about a week, to mix a little of the new food in with the old, increasing the proportion of new to old as the days progress. At the end of the week, you'll be feeding his regular portions of the new food, and he will barely notice the change.

these standards and prove this by listing the ingredients contained in the food on every package or can. The ingredients are listed in descending order, with the main ingredient listed first.

Through centuries of domestication, we have made our dogs entirely dependent upon us for their well-being. Therefore we are entirely responsible for duplicating the food balance that the wild dog finds in nature. The domesticated dog's diet must include protein, carbohydrates, fats, roughage and small amounts of essential minerals and vitamins. Finding commercially prepared diets that contain all of the necessary nutrients will not present a problem. A visit to your local supermarket or pet store will reveal the vast array from which you will be able to select. Among the many varieties of dog foods are canned, dry, semi-moist, "scientifically fortified," "all-natural"—and the list goes on. Fresh water and a properly prepared balanced diet that contains the essential nutrients in correct proportions are all that a healthy Caucasian Mountain Dog needs to be offered.

DIET DON'TS

- Got milk? Don't give it to your dog! Dogs cannot tolerate large quantities of cow's milk, as they do not have the enzymes to digest lactose.
- You may have heard of dog owners who add raw eggs to their dogs' food for a shiny coat or to make the food more palatable, but consumption of raw eggs too often can cause a deficiency of the vitamin biotin.
- Avoid feeding table scraps, as they will upset the balance of the dog's complete food. Additionally, fatty or highly seasoned foods can cause upset canine stomachs.
- Do not offer raw meat to your dog. Raw meat can contain parasites; it also is high in fat.
- Vitamin A toxicity in dogs can be caused by too much raw liver, especially if the dog already gets enough vitamin A in his balanced diet, which should be the case.
- Bones like chicken, pork chop and other soft bones are not suitable, as they easily splinter.

It is important to remember that all dogs, whether they are Chihuahuas, Great Danes or anything in between, are carnivorous (meat-eating) animals. While the vegetable content of your Caucasian Mountain Dog's diet should not be overlooked, a dog's physiology and anatomy are based upon carnivorous food acquisition. Protein and fat are absolutely essential to the well-being of your dog. In fact, it is wise to add a teaspoon or two of vegetable oil or bacon drippings to your dog's diet, particularly during the winter months in colder climates.

It is also important to understand that commercially prepared dog foods do contain all of the nutrients that your Caucasian Mountain Dog needs. It is therefore unnecessary to add vitamin supplements to these diets except in special circumstances prescribed by your breeder or veterinarian. It is essential not to supplement this fast-growing breed with excess calcium and phosphorus, as such a practice can result in skeletal growth problems and exacerbate any genetic tendency to hip dysplasia.

A great deal of controversy exists today regarding orthopedic problems such as hip dysplasia and patellar (knee) luxation that can afflict all breeds. Some claim that these problems are entirely hereditary conditions, but many others feel that these problems can be exacerbated by overuse of mineral and vitamin supplements for puppies.

There are now any number of commercially prepared diets for dogs with special dietary needs. The overweight, underweight or geriatric dog can have his nutritional needs met, as can puppies and growing dogs. The calorie content of each of these foods is adjusted accordingly. With the correct amount of the right foods and the proper amount of exercise, your Caucasian Mountain Dog should stay in top shape. Again, common sense must prevail. Too many calories will increase weight and cutting back on calories will reduce weight.

A hungry Caucasian will find his food!

NOT HUNGRY?

No dog in his right mind would turn down his dinner, would he? If you notice that your dog has lost interest in his food, there could be any number of causes. Dental problems are a common cause of appetite loss, one that is often overlooked. If your dog has a toothache, a loose tooth or sore gums from infection, chances are it doesn't feel so good to chew. Think about when you've had a toothache! If your dog does not approach the food bowl with his usual enthusiasm, look inside his mouth for signs of a problem. Whatever the cause, you'll want to consult your vet so that your chow hound can get back to his happy, hungry self as soon as possible.

Fed with any regularity at all, refined sugars can cause your Caucasian Mountain Dog to become obese and will definitely create tooth decay. Candy stores do not exist in the wild and canine teeth are not genetically disposed to handling sugars. Do not feed your Caucasian Mountain Dog candy or sweets, and avoid products that contain sugar to any high degree. Chocolate is actually toxic to dogs, along with grapes, raisins, nuts and onions.

Occasionally, a young Caucasian Mountain Dog going through the teething period or a female coming into season will go "off" his or her food. The concerned owner's first response often is to tempt the dog by hand-feeding special treats and foods that the problem eater seems to prefer. This practice only serves to compound the problem. Once a dog learns to play the waiting game, he will turn up his nose at anything other than his favorite food, knowing full well that what he wants to eat will eventually arrive.

Because your Caucasian's food has a bearing on coat, health and temperament, it is essential that the most suitable diet is selected for your dog and his stage of life. It is fair to say, however, that even experienced owners can be perplexed by the enormous range of foods available. Only understanding what is best for your dog will help you reach an informed decision. When selecting your dog's diet, three stages of development must be considered: the puppy stage, the adult stage and the senior stage.

FEEDING THE PUPPY
By the time the puppies are seven or a maximum of eight weeks old, they should be fully weaned and fed solely on a proprietary puppy food. Selection of the most suitable, good-quality diet at this time is essential, for a puppy's fastest growth rate is during the first year of life. Your vet and breeder should be able to offer good advice in this regard. The frequency of meals will be reduced over time, and the transition from growth-formula food to an adult-maintenance diet can begin at any time after the pup reaches ten months of age. Puppies should be fed moderate

amounts of a moderate protein food with controlled mineral content (commercially available).

ADULT DIETS
In the Caucasian Mountain Dog, full size comes early, at about nine or ten months of age, while full maturity comes later. Depending upon the individual dog and his general condition (weight, activity level, etc.), the maintenance diet can be used with most Caucasian Mountain Dogs until around eight years of age or even older.

Again you should rely upon your vet and breeder to recommend an acceptable maintenance diet. Major dog-food manufacturers specialize in this type of food, and it is merely necessary for you to select the one best suited to your dog's needs. For example, active dogs will have different requirements from those of dogs who live more sedentary lives.

SENIOR DIETS
As dogs get older, their metabolism changes. The older dog usually exercises less, moves more slowly and sleeps more. This change in lifestyle and physiological performance requires a change in diet. Since these changes take place slowly, they might not be recognizable. What is easily recognizable is weight gain. By continuing to feed your dog an adult-maintenance diet when he is slowing down meta-

bolically, your dog will gain weight. Obesity in an older dog compounds the health problems that already accompany old age.

As your dog gets older, few of his organs function up to par. The kidneys slow down and the intestines become less efficient. These age-related factors are best handled with a change in diet and a change in feeding schedule to give smaller portions that are more easily digested. Eight years old might be the average age at which to consider a Caucasian Mountain Dog as a "senior" and to consult your vet about changing your dog's diet. There is no single best diet for every older dog. While many dogs do well on light or senior diets, other dogs do better on other special premium diets such as lamb and rice. Be sensitive to your senior Caucasian Mountain Dog's diet, as this will help control other problems that may arise with your old friend.

DON'T FORGET THE WATER!

Regardless of what type of food your Caucasian eats, there's no doubt that he needs plenty of water. Fresh cold water, in a clean bowl, should be made available to your dog. There are special circumstances, such as during puppy housebreaking, when you will want to monitor your pup's water intake so that you will be able to predict when he will need to relieve himself, but water must

Treats are helpful tools in teaching and rewarding your Caucasian, but don't overdo it. Consider how many treats you give your dog when figuring out his daily food portions.

be available to him nonetheless. Water is essential for hydration and proper body function just as it is in humans.

You will get to know how much your dog typically drinks in a day. Of course, in the heat or if exercising vigorously, he will be more thirsty and will drink more. However, if he begins to drink noticeably more water for no apparent reason, this could signal any of various problems, and you are advised to consult your vet.

A word of caution concerning your deep-chested Caucasian's water intake: he should never be allowed to gulp water, especially at mealtimes. In fact, his water should be limited or even

WEIGHT AND SEE!

When you look at yourself in the mirror each day, you get very used to what you see! It's only when you pull out last year's vacation outfit and can't zip it up that you notice that you've put on some pounds. Dog owners are the same way with their dogs. Often a few pounds go unnoticed, and it's not until some time passes or the vet remarks that your dog looks more than pleasantly plump that you realize what's happened. To avoid your pet's becoming obese right under your very nose, make a habit of routinely evaluating his condition with a hands-on test.

Can you feel, but not see, your dog's rib cage? Does your dog have a waist? His waist should be evident by touch and also visible from above and from the side. In top view, the dog's body should have an hourglass shape. These are indicators of good condition, often easier seen than felt with the heavily coated Caucasian.

While it's not hard to spot an extremely skinny or overly rotund dog, it's the subtle changes that lead up to under- or overweight condition of which we must be aware. If your dog's ribs are protruding, he is too thin. Conversely, if you can't feel the ribs under too much fat, and if there's no indication of a waistline, your dog is overweight. Both of these conditions require changes to the diet. A trip or sometimes just a call to the vet will help you modify your dog's feeding.

removed at mealtimes as a rule. This simple daily precaution can go a long way in protecting your dog from the dangerous and potentially fatal gastric torsion (bloat), explained in more detail in the health chapter.

EXERCISE

The Caucasian Mountain Dog has spent his existence walking with the grazing sheep, and walking is still the best exercise for the breed. At least one to two hours per day of exercise and activity, allowing plenty of time to rest between exercise periods and mealtimes, will keep your dog in proper condition. Keep in mind, however, that puppies should not be "road worked" or forced to exercise, as their fast-growing limbs and ligaments should not be stressed.

Daily long leash walks at a steady pace will help adult dogs of this breed develop and maintain proper musculature. Within reason, most anything you can do, your Caucasian Mountain Dog can do. Long morning walks, hikes over mountain trails, hiking, swimming and all outdoor activities—your Caucasian Mountain Dog will enjoy and benefit from these activities as much as you will. Free roaming in a securely fenced yard or farm is ideal.

Slow steady exercise that keeps your canine companion's heart rate in the working area will help to extend and improve the quality of his life. If your Caucasian Mountain Dog is getting his exercise with you at his side, you are increasing the chances that the two of you will enjoy each other's company for many more years to come.

Naturally, common sense must be used regarding the extent and intensity of the exercise you give your Caucasian Mountain Dog, especially the puppy. No puppy of any breed should be forced to accompany you on extended runs or to overdo it in any way. Serious injuries can result. Short exercise periods and long rest stops are best for any Caucasian Mountain Dog under 12 months of age.

Cold weather, even temperatures hovering around the zero-degree mark, are no problem at all

The puppy coat can be brushed in gentle strokes with a soft slicker brush.

for the Caucasian Mountain Dog. The only warm clothing required for your winter walks will be yours—as long as the two of you keep moving! Do not, however, allow your Caucasian Mountain Dog to remain wet if the two of you get caught in the rain or snow.

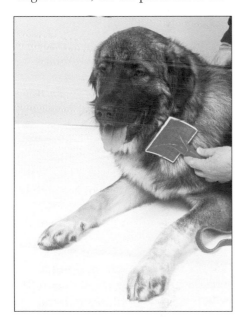

GROOMING

The Caucasian Mountain Dog should be groomed to look very natural, but not unkempt, and about 30–45 minutes per week are required to keep the breed in beautiful condition. Start the weekly grooming session by checking the eyes and ears for discharge. If a black discharge or foul smell is detected in the ears, ear mites or yeast infection may be the culprit.

A slicker brush is effective on the adult Caucasian's coat as well, but make sure the teeth are long enough to reach all the way to the skin.

This will require veterinary attention. Healthy ears should be cleaned with a cotton pad and either a vinegar and water solution or a commercial preparation.

Next, move on to the coat. Using a slicker or rubber cushioned pin brush, start systematically brushing layer by layer against the growth of coat. Have a spray bottle with water in it. Keep the coat slightly misted while brushing to help keep the coat

EYE CARE

During grooming sessions, pay extra attention to the condition of your dog's eyes. If the area around the eyes is soiled or if tear staining has occurred, there are various cleaning agents made especially for this purpose. Look at the dog's eyes to make sure no debris has entered; dogs with large eyes and those who spend time outdoors are especially prone to this.

The signs of an eye infection are obvious: mucus, redness, puffiness, scabs or other signs of irritation. If your dog's eyes become infected, the vet will likely prescribe an antibiotic ointment for treatment. If you notice signs of more serious problems, such as opacities in the eye, which usually indicate cataracts, consult the vet at once. Taking time to pay attention to your dog's eyes will alert you in the early stages of any problem so that you can get your dog treatment as soon as possible. You could save your dog's sight!

from breaking and also the undercoat from flying about. Brush all the way to the skin. Shampoo occasionally with an appropriate shampoo followed by a good conditioner. Avoid too-frequent baths, as they will dry the skin and cause the undercoat to blow out too often.

As needed, scissor around the feet to give a more compact look. Thinning shears can be used to shape up the tops of the feet by brushing the hair upward and lightly trimming off uneven or bulky hair. Scissor with the lay of hair. Tidy up the hock area the same way, by combing the hair straight out from the hocks and evening up the hair. Pasterns can also be trimmed the same way.

Depending on climate, the Caucasian Mountain Dog sheds year-round with a once- or twice-annual molt. Breeders commonly call this shedding process "blowing the coat." A portable high-speed air blower, available through dog-grooming or pet-supply catalogs, is very useful during seasonal molts to quickly remove quantities of undercoat.

BATHING

In general, dogs need to be bathed only a few times a year, possibly more often if your dog gets into something messy or if he starts to smell like a dog. Show dogs are usually bathed before every show, although this depends on the owner. As we've mentioned, bathing too frequently can have negative effects on the skin and coat, removing natural oils and causing dryness.

If you give your dog his first bath when he is young, he will become accustomed to the process. Struggling with an adult Caucasian or chasing a freshly shampooed dog who has escaped from the bath will be no fun! Most dogs don't naturally enjoy their baths, but you at least want yours to cooperate with you.

Before bathing the dog, have the items you'll need close at hand. First, decide where you will bathe the dog. You should have a tub or basin with a non-slip surface. In warm weather, some like to use a portable pool in the yard, although you'll want to make sure your dog doesn't head for the nearest dirt pile following his bath! You will also need a hose or shower spray to wet the coat thoroughly, a shampoo formulated for dogs, absorbent towels and perhaps a blow dryer. Human shampoos are too harsh for dogs' coats and will dry them out.

Before wetting the dog, give him a brush-through to remove any dead hair, dirt and mats. Make sure he is at ease in the tub and have the water at a comfortable temperature. Begin bathing by wetting the coat all the way down to the skin. Massage in the shampoo, keeping it away from

THE EARS KNOW
Examining your puppy's ears helps ensure good internal health. The ears are the eyes to the dog's innards! Begin handling and cleaning your puppy's ears when he's still young so that he doesn't protest every time you lift a flap or touch his ears. Yeast and bacteria are two of the culprits that you can detect by examining the ear. You will notice a strong, often foul, odor, debris, redness or some kind of discharge. All of these point to health problems that can worsen over time. Additionally, you are on the lookout for wax accumulation, ear mites and other tiny bothersome parasites and their even tinier droppings. You may have to pluck hair with tweezers in order to have a better view into the dog's ears, but this is painless if done carefully.

his face and eyes. Rinse him thoroughly, again avoiding the eyes and ears, as you don't want to get water into the ear canals. A thorough rinsing is important, as shampoo residue is drying and

Completely at ease for his pedicure! The key to having an adult Caucasian who cooperates with grooming tasks is to start when the pup is young.

distance from the dog or an air blower made for grooming. You should keep the dog indoors and away from drafts until he is completely dry.

NAIL CLIPPING

Toenails should be kept short enough to clear the ground to prevent splayed feet. Also, you should always inspect your dog's feet for cracked pads. Check between the toes for splinters and thorns. Pay particular attention to any swollen or tender areas.

The nails of a Caucasian Mountain Dog who spends most of his time indoors or on grass when outdoors can grow long very quickly. Do not allow the nails to become overgrown and then expect to cut them back easily. Each nail has a blood vessel running through the center called the "quick." The quick grows close to the end of the nail and contains very sensitive nerve endings. If the nail is allowed to grow too long, it will be impossible to cut it back to a proper length without cutting into the quick. This causes severe pain to the dog and can also result in a great deal of bleeding that can be very difficult to stop. A good rule of thumb is that it's time to trim when you can hear the dog's nails clicking on the floor or pavement.

This Caucasian knows the routine and gives his paw to have his nails clipped.

itchy to the dog. After rinsing, wrap him in a towel to absorb the initial moisture. You can finish drying with a towel, a blow dryer on low heat held at a safe

If your Caucasian Mountain Dog is getting plenty of exercise on cement or rough hard pavement, the nails may be kept sufficiently worn down. Otherwise, the nails can grow long very quickly and must then be trimmed with canine nail clippers, an electric nail grinder or a coarse file made expressly for that purpose. All three of these items can be purchased at pet stores. Regardless of which nail-trimming device is used, proceed with caution and remove only a small portion of the nail at time. Should the quick be nipped in the trimming process,

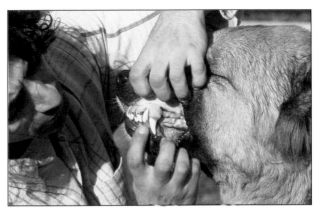

there are a number of blood-clotting products (such as styptic powder or pencil, as used for shaving) available at pet shops that will almost immediately stem the flow of blood. It is wise to have one of these products on hand in case there is a nail-trimming accident or the dog tears a nail on his own.

IDENTIFICATION AND TRAVEL

ID FOR YOUR DOG

You love your Caucasian and want to keep him safe. Of course, you take every precaution to prevent his escaping from the yard or becoming lost or stolen. You have a sturdy high fence and you always keep your dog on lead when out and about in public places. If your dog is not properly identified, however, you are overlooking a major aspect of his safety. We hope to never be in a situation where our dog is missing, but we should practice prevention in the unfortunate case

Examining your dog's teeth and mouth, and brushing your dog's teeth at least once weekly (more often is even better) with doggie dental-care products must be part of your routine for your Caucasian Mountain Dog's overall good health.

SCOOTING HIS BOTTOM

Here's a doggy problem that many owners tend to neglect. If your dog is scooting his rear end around the carpet, he probably is experiencing anal-sac impaction or blockage. The anal sacs are the two grape-sized glands on either side of the dog's vent. The dog cannot empty these glands, which become filled with a foul-smelling material. The dog may attempt to lick the area to relieve the pressure. He may also rub his anus on your walls, furniture or floors.

Don't neglect your dog's rear end during grooming sessions. By squeezing both sides of the anus with a soft cloth, you can express some of the material in the sacs. If the material is pasty and thick, you likely will need the assistance of a veterinarian. Vets know how to express the glands and can show you how to do it correctly without hurting the dog or spraying yourself with the contents.

PET OR STRAY?

Besides the obvious benefit of providing your contact information to whoever finds your lost dog, an ID tag makes your dog more approachable and more likely to be recovered. A strange dog wandering the neighborhood without a collar and tags will look like a stray, while the collar and tags indicate that the dog is someone's pet. Even if the ID tags become detached from the collar, the collar alone will make a person more likely to pick up the dog.

that this happens; identification greatly increases the chances of your dog's being returned to you.

There are several ways to identify your dog. First, the traditional dog tag should be a staple in your dog's wardrobe, attached to his everyday collar. Tags can be made of sturdy plastic and various metals and should include your contact information so that a person who finds the dog can get in touch with you right away to arrange his return. Many people today enjoy the wide range of decorative tags available, so have fun and create a tag to match your dog's personality. Of course, it is important that the tag stays on the collar, so have a secure "O" ring attachment; you also can explore the type of tag that slides right onto the collar.

In addition to the ID tag, which every dog should wear

Your Caucasian's ID tags and necessary licenses should be securely attached to his everyday collar.

even if identified by another method, two other forms of identification have become popular: microchipping and tattooing. In microchipping, a tiny scannable chip is painlessly inserted under the dog's skin. The number is registered to you so that, if your lost dog turns up at a clinic or shelter, the chip can be scanned to retrieve your contact information.

The advantage of the microchip is that it is a permanent form of ID, but there are some factors to consider. Several different companies make microchips, and not all are compatible with the others' scanning devices. It's best to find a company with a universal microchip that can be read by scanners made by other companies as well. It won't do any good to have the dog chipped if the information cannot be retrieved. Also, not every humane society, shelter and clinic is equipped with a scanner, although

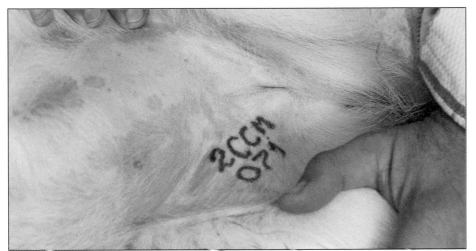

The light skin on the belly is a good place for an ID tattoo, as the markings are clearly visible.

more and more facilities are equipping themselves. In fact, many shelters microchip dogs that they adopt out to new homes.

In the US, there are five or six major microchip manufacturers as well as a few databases. Because the microchip is not visible to the eye, the dog must wear a tag that states that he is microchipped so that whoever picks him up will know to have him scanned. He of course also should have a tag with contact information in case his chip cannot be read. Humane societies and veterinary clinics offer this service, which is usually very affordable.

Though less popular than microchipping, tattooing is another permanent method of ID for dogs. Most vets perform this service, and there are also clinics that perform dog tattooing. This is also an affordable procedure and one that

will not cause much discomfort for the dog. It is best to put the tattoo in a visible area, such as the ear or belly, to deter theft. It is sad to say that there are cases of dogs' being stolen and sold to research laboratories, but such laboratories will not accept tattooed dogs.

To ensure that the tattoo is effective in aiding your dog's return to you, the tattoo number must be registered with a national organization. That way, when someone finds a tattooed dog, a phone call to the registry will quickly match the dog with his owner.

HIT THE ROAD
Car travel with your Caucasian may be limited to necessity only, such as trips to the vet, or you may bring your dog along almost everywhere you go. This will depend much on your individual

dog and how he reacts to rides in the car. You can begin desensitizing your dog to car travel as a pup so that it's something that he's used to. Still, some dogs suffer from motion sickness. Your vet may prescribe a medication for this if trips in the car pose a problem for your dog. At the very least, you will need to get him to the vet, so he will need to tolerate these trips with the least amount of hassle possible.

Start taking your pup on short trips, maybe just around the block to start. If he is fine with short trips, lengthen your rides a little at a time. Start to take him on your

errands or just for drives around town. By this time, it will be easy to tell whether your dog is a born traveler or would prefer staying at home when you are on the road.

Of course, safety is a concern for dogs in the car. First, he must travel securely, not left loose to roam about the car where he could be injured or distract the driver. A young pup can be held by a passenger initially, but your Caucasian will be too large for that before long. He should soon graduate to a travel crate, which can be the same crate he uses in the home if your vehicle is large enough. Other options include a car harness (like a seat belt for dogs) and partitioning the back of the car with a gate made for this purpose.

Bring along what you will need for the dog. He should wear his collar and ID tags, of course, and you should bring his leash, water (and food if a long trip) and clean-up materials for potty breaks and in case of motion sickness. Always keep your dog on his leash when you make stops, and never leave him alone in the car. Many a dog has died from the heat inside a closed car; this does not take much time at all in any kind of warm weather. Temperatures can soar in a matter of minutes and your Caucasian Mountain Dog can die of heat exhaustion in less time than you would ever imagine. Rolling down the windows helps little and is dangerous in that an

With a dog the size of the Caucasian, you will need a large vehicle to transport him. This dog travels in his own section of the family van, with the back partitioned to create a safe space for him.

overheated dog will panic and attempt to escape through the open window. A dog left alone inside a car can also be a target for thieves.

BOARDING

Today there are many options for dog owners who need someone to care for their dogs in certain circumstances. While many think of boarding their dogs as something to do when away on vacation, many others use the services of doggie "daycare" facilities, dropping their dogs off to spend the day while they are at work. Many of these facilities offer both long-term and daily care. Many go beyond just boarding and cater to all sorts of needs, with on-site grooming, veterinary care, training classes and even "web-cams" where owners can log onto the Internet and check out what their dogs are up to. Most dogs enjoy the activity and time spent with other dogs.

Before you need to use such a service, check out the ones in your area. Make visits to see the facilities, meet the staff, discuss fees and available services and see whether this is a place where you think your dog will be happy. Do they have ample experience with large breeds and plenty of room? Make it clear that your Caucasian may be aggressive toward other dogs and may take some time to warm up to the staff. It is best to do your research in advance so that you're not stuck at the last

minute, forced into making a rushed decision without knowing whether the kennel that you've chosen meets your standards. You also can check with your vet's office to see whether they offer boarding for their clients or can recommend a good kennel in the area. For Caucasian owners, boarding with their breeder or another Caucasian breeder might be the best option if he offers this service. This way, you know that your dog will be in the hands of someone who knows the breed.

The kennel will need to see proof of your dog's health records and vaccinations so as not to spread illness from dog to dog. Your dog also will need proper identification. Owners usually experience some separation anxiety the first time they have to leave their dog in someone else's care, so it's reassuring to know that the kennel you choose is run by experienced, caring, true dog people.

Is the boarding kennel clean, spacious and professionally run? Is it conveniently located? Is it affordable? Does the staff know how to handle a Caucasian properly? These are some of the questions to ask yourself when choosing a place to board your dog.

TRAINING YOUR

CAUCASIAN MOUNTAIN DOG

The Caucasian Mountain Dog is a freethinker! He is not one to revel in mindless repetition of the basic commands. He responds to positive reinforcement and encouragement, and he admires a trainer who knows what he wants. With a Caucasian, you must be prepared to train him in the most specific, direct manner possible. If you are a beginner, you may bore your Caucasian Mountain Dog to sleep. You have been forewarned.

While this is a most intelligent breed (perhaps a bit too smart at times), it can be a challenge to train. You, as the master and trainer, must impress upon your self-possessing puppy that you are the alpha because you are bigger, stronger and smarter! Obviously, you want to make this impression as soon as possible—before your Caucasian is the size of a little bear and less likely to be impressed by your mere human frame.

The author believes that the best way to obedience train your Caucasian is to enroll him in an obedience class. The instructor and the presence of other owners and their dogs will add to your dog's

socialization experiences while teaching your dog basic behaviors. The class is helpful for you, too. You will be able to teach your dog good manners as you learn how and why he behaves the way he does. You will find out how to communicate with your dog and how to recognize and understand his communications with you.

There's a big difference between training an adult dog and training a young puppy. With a young puppy, everything is new. At nine or so weeks of age, he will be experiencing many things, and he has nothing with which to compare these experiences. Up to this point, he has been with his dam and littermates, not one-on-one with people except in his interactions with his breeder and visitors to the litter.

When you first bring the puppy home, he is eager to please you. This means that he accepts doing things your way. During the next couple of months, he will absorb the basis of everything he needs to know for the rest of his life. This early age is even referred to as the "sponge" stage. After that, for the next 18 months, it's up to you to reinforce good manners by building on the foundation that you've established. Of course, your reinforcement of his good manners will be ongoing for his whole life. Once your puppy is reliable in basic commands and behavior and has reached the appropriate age, you may gradually introduce him to some of the interesting canine sports, games and activities.

Raising your puppy is a family affair. Each member of the family must know what rules to set forth for the puppy and how to use the same one-word commands to mean exactly the same thing every time. Even if yours is a large family, one person will soon be considered by the pup to be the leader, the alpha person in his pack, the "boss" who must be obeyed. Often that highly regarded person turns out to be the one who feeds the puppy. Food ranks very high on the puppy's list of important things! That's why your puppy is rewarded with small treats along with verbal praise when he responds to you correctly. As the puppy learns to do what you want him to do, the food rewards are gradually eliminated and only the praise remains. If you were to keep up with the food treats, you could have two problems on your hands—an obese dog and a beggar.

Training begins the minute your Caucasian puppy steps

SHOULD WE ENROLL?

If you have the means and the time, you should definitely take your dog to obedience classes. Begin with Puppy Kindergarten classes in which puppies of all sizes learn basic lessons while getting the opportunity to meet and greet each other; it's as much about socialization as it is about good manners. What you learn in class, you can practice at home. And if you goof up in practice, you'll get help in the next session.

through the doorway of your home, so don't make the mistake of putting the puppy on the floor and telling him by your actions to "Go for it! Run wild!" Even if this is your first puppy, you must act as if you know what you're doing: be the boss. An uncertain pup may be

LEADER OF THE PACK

Canines are pack animals. They live according to pack rules, and every pack has only one leader. Guess what? That's you! To establish your position of authority, lay down the rules and be fair and good-natured in all your dealings with your dog. He will consider young children as his littermates, but the one who trains him, who feeds him, who grooms him, who expects him to come into line, that's his leader. And he who leads must be obeyed.

It's worth mentioning here that if you've adopted an adult dog that is completely trained to your liking, lucky you! You're off the hook! However, if that dog spent his life up to this point in a kennel, or even in a good home but without any real training, be prepared to tackle the job ahead. A dog three years of age or older with no previous training cannot be blamed for not knowing what he was never taught. While the dog is trying to understand and learn your rules, at the same time he has to unlearn many of his previously self-taught habits and general view of the world. It can be difficult to train and socialize an adult Caucasian, but it is possible.

terrified to move, while a bold one will be ready to take you at your word and start plotting to destroy the house! Before you collected your puppy, you decided where his own special place would be, and that's where to put him when you first arrive home. Give him a house tour after he has investigated his area and had a nap and a bathroom "pit stop."

Working with a trainer who knows the breed will be a big help in making progress with an adopted adult dog and is certainly advised. You'll need patience, too. Some new rules may be close to impossible for the dog to accept. After all, he's been successful so far by doing everything his way! (Patience again.) He may agree with your instruction for a few days and then slip back into his old ways, so you must be just as consistent and understanding in your teaching as you would be with a puppy. (More patience needed yet again!) Your dog has to learn to pay attention to your voice, your family, the daily routine, new smells, new sounds and, in some cases, even a new climate.

With a unique dog like the Caucasian, you'll need a unique approach to training based on the breed's temperament and your dog's personality.

One of the most important things to find out about a newly adopted adult Caucasian is his reaction to children (yours and others), strangers and your friends, and how he acts upon meeting other dogs. These meetings must be done extremely carefully. If he was not socialized with dogs as a puppy, this could be a major problem. This does not mean that he's a vicious dog; rather, it means that he has no idea how to read another dog's body language. There's no way for him to tell whether the other dog is a friend or foe. His innate protection instinct takes over, telling him to attack first and ask questions later. This definitely calls for professional help and, even then, may not be a behavior that can be corrected 100% reliably (or even at all). If you have a puppy, this is why it is so very important to introduce your young Caucasian properly to other

Ready to get started? Let's shake on it! Don't forget that you and your dog are partners in the training process.

puppies and "dog-friendly" adult dogs.

Most likely you will be able to find obedience classes within a reasonable distance from your home, and the cost for such classes should be reasonably affordable. At home, too, you will want to reinforce your Caucasian's ever-growing education with some homework. Every instructor teaches the basic commands somewhat differently, but all approaches generally revolve around the simple principles of positive reinforcement. Caucasian respond best to inducive training and lots of "Good dog" praise. Now let us get started with some basic training for the home.

HOUSE-TRAINING YOUR CAUCASIAN

Dogs are tactility-oriented when it comes to house-training. In other words, they respond to the surface on which they are given approval to eliminate. The choice is yours (the dog's version is in parenthe-

TEACHER'S PET
Dogs are individuals, not robots, with many traits basic to their breed. Some, bred to work alone, are independent thinkers; others rely on you to call the shots. If you have enrolled in a training class, your instructor can offer alternative methods of training based on your individual dog's instincts and personality. You may benefit from using a different type of collar or switching to a class with different kinds of dogs.

ses): The lawn (including the neighbors' lawns)? A bare patch of earth under a tree (where people like to sit and relax in the summertime)? Concrete steps or patio (all sidewalks, garages and basement floors)? The curbside (watch out for cars)? A small area of crushed stone in a corner of the yard (mine!)? The latter is the best choice if you can manage it,

---

DAILY SCHEDULE

How many relief trips does your puppy need per day? A puppy up to the age of 14 weeks will need to go outside about 8 to 12 times per day! You will have to take the pup out any time he starts sniffing around the floor or turning in small circles, as well as after naps, meals, games and lessons or whenever he's released from his crate. Once the puppy is 14 to 22 weeks of age, he will require only 6 to 8 relief trips. At the ages of 22 to 32 weeks, the puppy will require about 5 to 7 trips. Adult dogs typically require 4 relief trips per day, in the morning, afternoon, evening and late at night.

---

because it will remain strictly for the dog's use and is easy to keep clean.

WHEN YOUR PUPPY'S "GOT TO GO"
Your puppy's need to relieve himself is seemingly non-stop, but signs of improvement will be seen each week. From 9 to 10 weeks old, the puppy will have to be taken outside every time he wakes up, about 10–15 minutes after every meal and after every period of play—all day long, from first thing in the morning until his bedtime! That's a total of ten or more trips per day to teach the puppy where it's okay to relieve himself. With that schedule in mind, you can see that house-training a young puppy is not a part-time job. It requires someone to be home all day.

If that seems overwhelming or impossible, do a little planning. For example, plan to pick up your puppy at the start of a vacation period. If you can't get home in the middle of the day, plan to hire a dog-sitter or ask a neighbor to come over to take the pup outside, feed him his lunch and then take him out again about ten or so minutes after he's eaten. Also make arrangements with that or another person to be your "emergency" contact if you have to stay late on the job. Remind yourself— repeatedly—that this hectic schedule improves as the puppy gets older.

CANINE DEVELOPMENT SCHEDULE

It is important to understand how and at what age a puppy develops into adulthood. If you are a puppy owner, consult the following Canine Development Schedule to determine the stage of development your puppy is currently experiencing. This knowledge will help you as you work with the puppy in the weeks and months ahead.

Period	Age	Characteristics
First to Third	Birth to Seven Weeks	Puppy needs food, sleep and warmth and responds to simple and gentle touching. Needs mother for security and disciplining. Needs littermates for learning and interacting with other dogs. Pup learns to function within a pack and learns pack order of dominance. Begin socializing pup with adults and children for short periods. Pup begins to become aware of his environment.
Fourth	Eight to Twelve Weeks	Brain is fully developed. Pup needs socializing with outside world. Remove from mother and littermates. Needs to change from canine pack to human pack. Human dominance necessary. Fear period occurs between 8 and 10 weeks. Avoid fright and pain.
Fifth	Thirteen to Sixteen Weeks	Training and formal obedience should begin. Less association with other dogs, more with people, places, situations. Period will pass easily if you remember this is pup's change-to-adolescence time. Be firm and fair. Flight instinct prominent. Permissiveness and over-disciplining can do permanent damage. Praise for good behavior.
Juvenile	Four to Eight Months	Another fear period about 7 to 8 months of age. It passes quickly, but be cautious of fright and pain. Sexual maturity reached. Dominant traits established. Dog should understand sit, down, come and stay by now.

NOTE: THESE ARE APPROXIMATE TIME FRAMES. ALLOW FOR INDIVIDUAL DIFFERENCES IN PUPPIES.

HOME WITHIN A HOME

Your Caucasian puppy needs to be confined to one secure, puppy-proof area when no one is able to watch his every move. Generally the kitchen is the place of choice because the floor is washable. Likewise, it's a busy family area that will accustom the pup to a variety of noises, everything from pots and pans to the telephone, blender and dishwasher. He will also be enchanted by the smell of your cooking (and will never be critical when you burn something). An exercise pen (also called an "ex-pen," a puppy version of a playpen) within the room of choice is an excellent means of confinement for a young pup. He can see out and has a certain amount of space in which to run about, but he is safe from dangerous things like electrical cords, heating units, trash baskets or open kitchen-supply cabinets. Place the pen where the puppy

A small carrier like this is much too small for house-training; the Caucasian pup will also outgrow it as a travel crate in no time. It's best to purchase a large wire crate, suitable for an adult Caucasian, for use inside the home.

> **EXTRA! EXTRA!**
> The headlines read: "Puppy Piddles Here!" Breeders commonly use newspapers to line their whelping pens, so puppies learn to associate newspapers with relieving themselves. Do not use newspapers to line your pup's crate, as this will signal to your puppy that it is OK to urinate in his crate.

will not get a blast of heat or air conditioning.

In the pen, you can put a few toys, his bed (which can be his crate if the dimensions of pen and crate are compatible) and a few layers of newspaper in one small corner, just in case. A water bowl can be hung at a convenient height on the side of the ex-pen so it won't become a splashing pool for an innovative puppy. His food dish can go on the floor, near but not under the water bowl.

Crates are something that pet owners are at last getting used to for their dogs. Wild or domestic canines have always preferred to sleep in den-like safe spots, and that is exactly what the crate provides. How often have you seen adult dogs that choose to sleep under a table or chair even though they have full run of the house? It's the den connection.

In your "happy" voice, use the word "Crate" every time you put the pup into his den. If he's new to a crate, toss in a small biscuit for

him to chase the first few times. At night, after he's been outside, he should sleep in his crate. The crate may be kept in his designated area at night or, if you want to be sure to hear those wake-up yips in the morning, put the crate in a corner of your bedroom. However, don't make any response whatsoever to whining or crying. If he's completely ignored, he'll settle down and get to sleep.

Good bedding for a young puppy is an old folded bath towel or an old blanket, something that is easily washable and disposable

A securely fenced yard provides the ideal house-training situation. With a trained adult, all you will have to do is let him out to do his business.

if necessary ("accidents" will happen!). Never put newspaper in the puppy's crate. Also, those old ideas about adding a clock to replace his mother's heartbeat, or a hot-water bottle to replace her warmth, are just that—old ideas. The clock could drive the puppy nuts, and the hot-water bottle could end up as a very soggy waterbed! An extremely good breeder would have introduced your puppy to the crate by letting two pups sleep together for a couple of nights, followed by several nights alone. How thankful you will be if you found that breeder!

Safe toys in the pup's crate or area will keep him occupied, but monitor their condition closely. Discard any toys that show signs of being chewed to bits. Squeaky parts, bits of stuffing or plastic or any other small pieces can cause

LEASH TRAINING

House-training and leash training go hand in hand, literally. When taking your puppy outside to do his business, lead him there on his leash. Unless an emergency potty run is called for, do not whisk the puppy up into your arms and take him outside. If you have a fenced yard, you have the advantage of letting the puppy loose to go out, but it's better to put the dog on the leash and take him to his designated place in the yard until he is reliably house-trained. Taking the puppy for a walk is the best way to house-train a dog. The dog will associate the walk with his time to relieve himself, and the exercise of walking stimulates the dog's bowels and bladder. Dogs that are not trained to relieve themselves on a walk may hold it until they get back home, which of course defeats half the purpose of the walk.

SOMEBODY TO BLAME

House-training a puppy can be frustrating for the puppy and the owner alike. The puppy does not instinctively understand the difference between defecating on the pavement outside and on the ceramic tile in the kitchen. He is confused and frightened by his human's exuberant reactions to his natural urges. The owner, arguably the more intelligent of the duo, is also frustrated that he cannot convince his puppy to obey his commands and instructions.

In frustration, the owner may struggle with the temptation to discipline the puppy, scold him or even strike him on the rear end. These harsh corrections are not only inappropriate but also will defeat your purpose in gaining your puppy's trust and respect. Don't blame your nine-week-old puppy. Blame yourself for not being 100% consistent in the puppy's lessons and routine. The lesson here is simple: try harder and your puppy will succeed.

intestinal blockage or possibly choking if swallowed.

PROGRESSING WITH POTTY-TRAINING
After you've taken your puppy out and he has relieved himself in the area you've selected, he can have some free time with the family as long as there is some-one responsible for watching him. That doesn't mean just someone in the same room who is watching TV or busy on the computer, but one person who is doing nothing other than keeping an eye on the pup, playing with him on the floor and helping him understand his position in the pack.

This first taste of freedom will let you begin to set the house rules. If you don't want the dog on the furniture, now is the time to prevent his first attempts to jump up onto the couch. The word to use in this case is "Off," not "Down."

Most corrections at this stage come in the form of simply distracting the puppy. Instead of telling him "No" for "Don't chew the carpet," distract the chomping puppy with a toy and he'll forget about the carpet.

As you are playing with the pup, do not forget to watch him closely and pay attention to his body language. Whenever you see him begin to circle or sniff, take the puppy outside to relieve himself. Praise him as he elimi-nates while he actually is *in the act* of relieving himself. Three seconds after he has finished is too late! You'll be praising him for running toward you, or picking up a toy or whatever he may be doing at that moment, and that's not what you want to be praising him for. Timing is a vital tool in all dog training. Use it.

If your pup has an accident in

the house, the scent will attract him to that spot when it's time to go again. That scent attraction is why it's so important to clean up any messes made in the house by using a product specially made to eliminate the odor of dog urine and droppings. Regular household cleansers won't do the trick. Pet shops sell the best pet deodorizers. Invest in the largest container you can find.

Scent attraction eventually will lead your pup to his chosen spot outdoors; this is the basis of outdoor training. When you take your puppy outside to relieve himself, use a one-word command such as "Outside" or "Go-potty" (that's one word to the puppy!) as you pick him up and attach his leash. Then put him down in his area. If for any reason you can't carry him, snap the leash on quickly and lead him to his spot. Now comes the hard part —hard for you, that is. Just stand there until he urinates and defecates. Move him a few feet in one direction or another if he's just sitting there looking at you, but remember that this is neither playtime nor time for a walk. This is strictly a business trip! Then, as he circles and squats (remember your timing!), give him a quiet "Good dog" as praise. If you start to jump for joy, ecstatic over his performance, he'll do one of two things: either he will stop midstream, as it were, or he'll do it

again for you—in the house—and expect you to be just as delighted!

Give him five minutes or so and, if he doesn't go in that time, take him back indoors to his confined area and try again in another ten minutes, or immediately if you see him sniffing and circling. By careful observation, you'll soon work out a successful schedule.

Accidents, by the way, are just that—accidents. Clean them up quickly and thoroughly, without comment, after the puppy has been taken outside to finish his business and then put back into his area or crate. If you witness an accident in progress, say "No!" in a stern voice and get the pup outdoors immediately. No punishment is needed. You and your puppy are just learning each other's language, and sometimes it's easy to miss a puppy's message. Chalk it up to experience and watch more closely from now on.

KEEPING THE PACK ORDERLY

Discipline is a form of training that brings order to life. For example, military discipline is what allows the soldiers in an army to work as one. Discipline is a form of teaching and, in dogs, is the basis of how the successful pack operates. Each member knows his place in the pack and all respect the leader, or alpha dog. It is essential for your puppy that you establish this type of relationship, with you as the alpha, or leader. It is a form of social coexistence that all canines recognize and accept. Discipline, therefore, is never to be confused with punishment. When you teach your puppy how you want him to behave, and he behaves properly and you praise him for it, you are disciplining him with a form of positive reinforcement.

For a dog, rewards come in the form of praise, a smile, a cheerful tone of voice, a few friendly pats or a rub of the ears. Rewards are also small food treats. Obviously, that does not mean bits of regular dog food. Instead, treats are very small bits of special things like cheese or pieces of soft dog treats. The idea is to reward the dog with something very small that he can taste and swallow, providing instant positive reinforcement. If he has to take time to chew the treat, by the time he is finished he will have forgotten what he did to earn it!

Your puppy should never be physically punished. The displeasure shown on your face and in your voice is sufficient to signal to the pup that he has done something wrong. He wants to please everyone higher up on the social ladder, especially his leader, so a scowl and harsh voice will take care of the error. Growling out the word "Shame!" when the pup is caught in the act of doing something wrong is better than the repetitive "No." Some dogs hear "No" so often that they begin to think it's their name! By the way, do not use the dog's name when you're correcting him. His name is reserved to get his attention for

POTTY COMMAND

Most dogs love to please their masters; there are no bounds to what dogs will do to make their owners happy. The potty command is a good example of this theory. If toileting on command makes the master happy, then more power to him. Puppies will obligingly piddle if it really makes their keepers smile. Some owners can be creative about which word they will use to command their dogs to relieve themselves. Some popular choices are "Potty," "Tinkle," "Piddle," "Let's go," "Hurry up" and "Toilet." Give the command every time your puppy goes into position and the puppy will begin to associate his business with the command.

something pleasant about to take place.

There are punishments that have nothing to do with you. For example, your dog may think that chasing cats is one reason for his existence. You can try to stop it as much as you like but without success, because it's such fun for the dog. But one good hissing, spitting swipe of a cat's claws across the dog's nose will put an end to the game forever. Intervene only when your dog's eyeball is seriously at risk. Cat scratches can cause permanent damage to an innocent but annoying puppy.

PUPPY KINDERGARTEN

Collar and Leash
Before you begin your Caucasian puppy's education, he must be used to his collar and leash.

A Caucasian pup is a bright, alert "sponge," ready to soak up the lessons that you teach him.

Choose a collar for your puppy that is secure, but not heavy or bulky. He won't enjoy training if he's uncomfortable. A flat buckle collar is fine for everyday wear and for initial puppy training. For older dogs, there are several types of training collars such as the martingale, which is a double loop that tightens slightly around the neck, or the head collar, which is similar to a horse's halter. Do not use a chain choke collar with a Caucasian, as it will damage his fur. If using another type of choke, you must be specifically shown how to put it on and how to use it, and do not use it with a puppy. Ask your breeder for advice about training collars.

A lightweight 6-foot woven cotton or nylon training leash is preferred by most trainers because it is easy to fold up in your hand

BASIC PRINCIPLES OF DOG TRAINING
1. Start training early. A young puppy is ready, willing and able.
2. Timing is your all-important tool. Praise at the exact time that the dog responds correctly. Pay close attention.
3. Patience is almost as important as timing!
4. Repeat! The same word has to mean the same thing every time.
5. In the beginning, praise all correct behavior verbally, along with treats and petting.

With a puppy, a sturdy yet lightweight buckle collar will suffice, taking into consideration that it must fit comfortably over his coat.

An adult Caucasian who pulls on the lead may do well with a head collar as a training collar.

and comfortable to hold because there is a certain amount of give to it. There are lessons where the dog will start off 6 feet away from you at the end of the leash. The leash used to take the puppy outside to relieve himself is shorter because you don't want him to roam away from his area. The shorter leash will also be the one to use when you walk the puppy.

If you've been wise enough to enroll in a Puppy Kindergarten training class, suggestions will be made as to the best collar and leash for your young puppy. I say "wise" because your puppy will be in a class with puppies in his age range (up to five months old) of all breeds and sizes. It's the perfect way for him to learn the right way (and the wrong way) to

interact with other dogs as well as their people. You cannot teach your puppy how to interpret another dog's sign language. For a first-time puppy owner, these socialization classes are invaluable. For experienced dog owners, they are a real boon to further training.

ATTENTION
You've been using the dog's name since the minute you collected him from the breeder, so you should be able to get his attention by saying his name—with a big smile and in an excited tone of voice. His response will be the puppy equivalent of "Here I am! What are we going to do?" Your immediate response (if you haven't guessed by now) is "Good dog." Rewarding him at the moment he pays attention to you teaches him the proper way to respond when he hears his name.

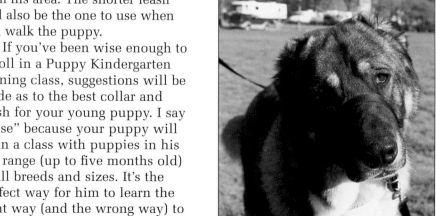

your hand. At that point, he will have to either sit or fall over, so as his back legs buckle under, say "Sit, good dog," and then give him the treat and lots of praise. You may have to begin with your hand lightly running up his chest, actually lifting his chin up until he sits. Some (usually older) dogs require gentle pressure on their hindquarters with the left hand, in which case the dog should be on your left side. Puppies generally do not appreciate this physical dominance.

The first step in training is getting the pup's attention, whether you use a toy, a treat or something else that he finds interesting.

EXERCISES FOR A BASIC CANINE EDUCATION

THE SIT EXERCISE

There are several ways to teach the puppy to sit. The first one is to catch him whenever he is about to sit and, as his backside nears the floor, say "Sit, good dog!" That's positive reinforcement and, if your timing is sharp, he will learn that what he's doing at that second is connected to your saying "Sit" and that you think he's clever for doing it!

Another method is to start with the puppy on his leash in front of you. Show him a treat in the palm of your right hand. Bring your hand up under his nose and, almost in slow motion, move your hand up and back so his nose goes up in the air and his head tilts back as he follows the treat in

A SIMPLE "SIT"
When you command your dog to sit, use the word "Sit." Do not say "Sit down," as your dog will not know whether you mean "Sit" or "Down," or maybe you mean both. Be clear in your instructions to your dog; use one-word commands and always be consistent.

After a few times, you should be able to show the dog a treat in the open palm of your hand, raise your hand waist-high as you say "Sit" and have him sit. You will thereby have taught him two things at the same time. Both the verbal command and the motion of the hand are signals for the sit. Your puppy is watching you almost more than he is listening to you, so what you do is just as important as what you say.

Don't save any of these drills only for training sessions. Use them as much as possible at odd times during a normal day. The dog should always sit before being given his food dish. He should sit to let you go through a doorway first, when the doorbell rings or when you stop to speak to someone on the street.

SMILE WHEN YOU ORDER ME AROUND!

While trainers recommend practicing with your dog every day, it's perfectly acceptable to take a "mental health day" off. It's better not to train the dog on days when you're in a sour mood. Your bad attitude or lack of interest will be sensed by your dog, and he will respond accordingly. Studies show that dogs are well tuned in to their humans' emotions. Be conscious of how you use your voice when talking to your dog. Raising your voice or shouting will only erode your dog's trust in you as his trainer and master.

THE DOWN EXERCISE

Before beginning to teach the down command, you must consider how the dog feels about this exercise. To him, "Down" is a submissive position. Being flat on the floor with you standing over him is not his idea of fun. It's up to you to let him know that, while it may not be fun, the reward of your approval is worth his effort.

Start with the puppy on your left side in a sit position. Hold the leash right above his collar in your left hand. Have an extra-special treat, such as a small piece of cooked chicken or hot dog, in your right hand. Place it at the end of the pup's nose and steadily move your hand down and forward along the ground. Hold the leash to prevent a sudden lunge for the food. As the puppy goes into the down position, say "Down" very gently.

The difficulty with this exercise is twofold: it's both the submissive aspect and the fact that most people say the word "Down" as if they were a drill sergeant in charge of recruits! So issue the command sweetly, give him the treat and have the pup maintain the down position for several seconds. If he tries to get up immediately, place your hands on his shoulders and press down gently, giving him a very quiet "Good dog." As you progress with this lesson, increase the "down time" until he will hold it until you say

"Okay" (his cue for release). Practice this one in the house at various times throughout the day.

By increasing the length of time during which the dog must maintain the down position, you'll find many uses for it. For example, he can lie at your feet in the vet's office or anywhere that both of you have to wait, when you are on the phone, while the family is eating and so forth. If you progress to training for competitive obedience, he'll already be all set for the exercise called the "long down."

THE STAY EXERCISE

You can teach your Caucasian to stay in the sit, down and stand positions. To teach the sit/stay, have the dog sit on your left side. Hold the leash at waist level in your left hand and let the dog know that you have a treat in your closed right hand. Step forward on your right foot as you say "Stay." Immediately turn and stand directly in front of the dog, keeping your right hand up high so he'll keep his eye on the treat hand and maintain the sit position for a count of five. Return to your original position and offer the reward.

Increase the length of the sit/stay each time until the dog can hold it for at least 30 seconds without moving. After about a week of success, move out on your right foot and take two steps

before turning to face the dog. Give the "Stay" hand signal (left palm back toward the dog's head) as you leave. He gets the treat when you return and he holds the sit/stay. Increase the distance that you walk away from him before turning until you reach the length of your training leash. But don't rush it! Go back to the beginning if he moves before he should. No matter what the lesson, never be upset by having to back up for a few days. The repetition and practice are what will make your dog reliable in these commands. It won't do any good to move on to something more difficult if the command is not mastered at the easier levels. Above all, even if you do get frustrated, never let your puppy know! Always keep a positive, upbeat attitude during training, which will transmit to your dog for positive results.

The down/stay is taught in the same way once the dog is completely reliable and steady

With an "alpha" breed like the Caucasian, trying to persuade him into a submissive position is not the easiest of tasks, but it can be accomplished with practice and a positive approach.

TIPS FOR TRAINING AND SAFETY

1. Whether on- or off-leash, practice only in a fenced area.
2. Remove the training collar when the training session is over.
3. Don't try to break up a dogfight.
4. "Come," "Leave it" and "Wait" are safety commands.
5. The dog belongs in a crate or behind a barrier when riding in the car.
6. Don't ignore the dog's first sign of aggression. Aggression only gets worse, so take it seriously.
7. Keep the faces of children and dogs separated.
8. Pay attention to what the dog is chewing.
9. Keep the vet's number near your phone.
10. "Okay" is a useful release command.

with the down command. Again, don't rush it. With the dog in the down position on your left side, step out on your right foot as you say "Stay." Return by walking around in back of the dog and into your original position. While you are training, it's okay to murmur something like "Hold on" to encourage him to stay put. When the dog will stay without moving when you are at a distance of 3 or 4 feet, begin to increase the length of time before you return. Be sure he holds the down on your return until you say "Okay." At that point, he gets his treat—just so

he'll remember for next time that it's not over until it's over.

THE COME EXERCISE

No command is more important to the safety of your Caucasian than "Come." It is what you should say every single time you see the puppy running toward you: "Binky, come! Good dog." During playtime, run a few feet away from the puppy and turn and tell him to "Come" as he is already running to you. You can go so far as to teach your puppy two things at once if you squat down and hold out your arms. As the pup gets close to you and you're saying "Good dog," bring your right arm in about waist high. Now he's also learning the hand signal, an excellent device should you be on the phone when you need to get him to come to you! You'll also both be one step ahead when you enter obedience classes.

When the puppy responds to your well-timed "Come," try it with the puppy on the training leash. This time, catch him off guard, while he's sniffing a leaf or watching a bird: "Binky, come!" You may have to pause for a split second after his name to be sure you have his attention. If the puppy shows any sign of confusion, give the leash a mild jerk and take a couple of steps backward. Do not repeat the command. In this case, you should say "Good come" as he reaches you.

That's the number-one rule of training. Each command word is given just once. Anything more is nagging. You'll also notice that all commands are one word only. Even when they are actually two words, you say them as one.

Never call the dog to come to you—with or without his name—if you are angry or intend to correct him for some misbehavior. When correcting the pup, you go to him. Your dog must always connect "Come" with something pleasant and with your approval; then you can rely on his response.

Puppies, like children, have notoriously short attention spans, so don't overdo it with any of the training. Keep each lesson short. Break it up with a quick run around the yard or a ball toss, repeat the lesson and quit as soon as the pup gets it right. That way, you will always end with a "Good dog."

Pups can learn from watching well-behaved adults. Here a youngster observes his first heeling lesson.

Life isn't perfect and neither are puppies. A time will come, often around ten months of age, when he'll become "selectively deaf" or choose to "forget" his name. He may respond by wagging his tail (and even seeming to smile at you) with a look that says "Make me!" Laugh, throw his favorite toy and skip the lesson you had planned. Pups will be pups!

THE HEEL EXERCISE

The second most important command to teach, after the come, is the heel. When you are walking your growing puppy, you need to be in control. Besides, it looks terrible to be pulled and yanked down the street, and it's not much fun either. Your nine-week-old puppy will probably follow you everywhere, but that's his natural instinct, not your control over the situation. However, any time he does follow you, you can say

---

LET'S GO!

Many people use "Let's go" instead of "Heel" when teaching their dogs to behave on lead. It sounds more like fun! When beginning to teach the heel, whatever command you use, always step off on your left foot. That's the one next to the dog, who is on your left side, in case you've forgotten. Keep a loose leash. When the dog pulls ahead, stop, bring him back and begin again. Use treats to guide him around turns.

"Heel" and be ahead of the game, as he will learn to associate this command with the action of following you before you even begin teaching him to heel.

There is a very precise, almost military, procedure for teaching your dog to heel. As with all other obedience training, begin with the dog on your left side. He will be in a very nice sit and you will have the training leash across your chest. Hold the loop and folded leash in your right hand. Pick up the slack leash above the dog in your left hand and hold it loosely at your side. Step out on your left foot as you say "Heel." If the puppy does not move, give a gentle tug or pat your left leg to get him started. If he surges ahead of you, stop and pull him back gently until he is at your side. Tell him to sit and begin again.

Walk a few steps and stop while the puppy is correctly beside you. Tell him to sit and give mild verbal praise. (More enthusiastic praise will encourage him to think the lesson is over.) Repeat the lesson, increasing the number of steps you take only as long as the dog is heeling nicely beside you. When you end the lesson, have him hold the sit and then give him the "Okay" to let him know that this is the end of the lesson. Praise him so that he knows he did a good job.

The cure for excessive pulling (a common problem) is to stop when the dog is no more than 2 or 3 feet ahead of you. Guide him back into position and begin again. With a really determined puller, try switching to a head collar. This will automatically turn the pup's head toward you so you can bring him back easily to the heel position. Give quiet, reassuring praise every time the leash goes slack and he's staying with you.

Staying and heeling can take a lot out of a dog, so provide playtime and free-running exercise to shake off the stress when the lessons are over. You don't want him to associate training with all work and no fun.

OTHER ACTIVITIES FOR LIFE

Whether a dog is trained in the structured environment of a class or alone with his owner at home, there are many activities that can bring fun and rewards to both owner and dog once they have mastered basic control.

NO MORE TREATS!

When your dog is responding promptly and correctly to commands, it's time to eliminate treats. Begin by alternating a treat reward with a verbal-praise-only reward. Gradually eliminate all treats while increasing the frequency of praise. Overlook pleading eyes and expectant expressions, but if he's still watching your treat hand, you're on your way to using hand signals.

Teaching the dog to help out around the home, in the yard or on the farm provides great satisfaction to both dog and owner. In addition, the dog's help makes life a little easier for his owner and raises his stature as a valued companion to his family. It helps give the dog a purpose by occupying his mind and providing an outlet for his energy. Caucasian Mountain Dogs are quick to learn and enjoy time spent with their owners. However, they have an independent streak and quickly become bored with everyday routine obedience training.

If you are interested in participating in organized competition with your Caucasian Mountain Dog, there are many activities in which you and your dog can become involved. At obedience trials, dogs can earn titles at various levels of competition. The beginning levels of obedience competition include basic behaviors such as sit, down, heel, etc. The more advanced levels of competition include jumping, retrieving, scent discrimination and signal work. The advanced levels require a dog and owner to put a lot of time and effort into their training. Caucasians have low prey drive, so fetch and retrieve exercises may be difficult to train. However, the titles that can be earned at these levels of competition are very prestigious if you progress to these levels with your Caucasian.

A Caucasian Mountain Dog owner must have control of her dog at all times, which is why having a dog that behaves well on lead is so important. A dog this size would be impossible to handle if not trained.

Agility is a popular sport in which dogs run through obstacle courses that include various jumps, tunnels and other exercises to test the dog's speed and coordination. The owners run beside their dogs to give commands and to guide them through the course. Caucasian Mountain Dogs are surefooted and may do well in agility if they can be motivated to participate.

The breed is naturally protective and has been used as guards for military installments and factories. Given the unique temperament of the breed, these protective traits are not easily applied to other disciplines. While individuals in the breed will exhibit different aptitudes, protection training sports such as Schutzhund are not recommended because the breed is very independent-minded and may not call off reliably.

HEALTHCARE OF YOUR

CAUCASIAN MOUNTAIN DOG

By Lowell Ackerman, DVM, DACVD

HEALTHCARE FOR A LIFETIME
When you own a dog, you become his healthcare advocate over his entire lifespan, as well as being the one to shoulder the financial burden of such care. Accordingly, it is worthwhile to focus on prevention rather than treatment, as you and your pet will both be happier.

Of course, the best place to have begun your program of preventive healthcare is with the initial purchase or adoption of your dog. There is no way of guaranteeing that your new furry friend is free of medical problems, but there are some things you can do to improve your odds. You certainly should have done adequate research into the Caucasian Mountain Dog and have selected your puppy carefully rather than buying on impulse. Health issues aside, a large number of pet abandonment and relinquishment cases arise from a mismatch between pet needs and owner expectations. This is entirely preventable with appropriate planning and finding a good breeder.

Regarding healthcare issues specifically, it is very difficult to make blanket statements about where to acquire a problem-free pet, but, again, a reputable breeder is your best bet. In an ideal situation, you have the opportunity to see both parents, get references from other owners of the breeder's pups and see genetic-testing documentation for several generations of the litter's ancestors. At the very least, you must thoroughly investigate the Caucasian Mountain Dog and the problems inherent in the breed, as well as the genetic testing available to screen for those problems. Genetic testing offers some important benefits, but testing is available for only a few disorders in a relatively small number of breeds and is not available for some of the most common genetic diseases, such as hip dysplasia, cataracts, epilepsy, cardiomyopathy, etc. This area of research is indeed exciting and increasingly important, and advances will continue to be made each year. In fact, recent research has shown that there is an equivalent dog gene for 75% of known human genes, so research done in either species is likely to benefit the other.

We've also discussed that evaluating the behavioral nature of your Caucasian Mountain Dog and that of his immediate family members is an important part of the selection process that cannot be underestimated or overemphasized. It is sometimes difficult to evaluate temperament in puppies because certain behavioral tendencies, such as some forms of aggression, may not be immediately evident. More dogs are euthanized each year for behavioral reasons than for all medical conditions combined, so it is critical to take temperament issues seriously. Start with a well-balanced, friendly companion and put the time and effort into proper socialization, and you will both be rewarded with a lifelong valued relationship.

Assuming that you have started off with a pup from healthy, sound stock, you then become responsible for helping your veterinarian keep your pet healthy. Some crucial things happen before you even bring your puppy home. Parasite control typically begins at two weeks of age, and vaccinations typically begin at six to eight weeks of age. A pre-pubertal evaluation is typically scheduled for about six months of age. At this time, a dental evaluation is done (since the adult teeth

> **DOGGIE DENTAL DON'TS**
>
> A veterinary dental exam is necessary if you notice one or any combination of the following in your dog:
> - Broken, loose or missing teeth
> - Loss of appetite (which could be due to mouth pain or illness caused by infection)
> - Gum abnormalities, including redness, swelling and bleeding
> - Drooling, with or without blood
> - Yellowing of the teeth or gumline, indicating tartar
> - Bad breath

are now in), heartworm prevention is started and neutering or spaying is most commonly done.

It is critical to commence regular dental care at home if you have not already done so. It may not sound very important, but most dogs have active periodontal disease by four years of age if they don't have their teeth cleaned regularly at home, not just at their veterinary exams. Dental problems lead to more than just bad "doggie breath." Gum disease can have very serious medical consequences. If you start brushing your dog's teeth and using antiseptic rinses from a young age, your dog will be accustomed to it and will not resist. The results will be healthy dentition, which your pet will need to enjoy a long, healthy life.

Most dogs are considered adults at around a year of age; with the Caucasian, full size is usually

reached by ten months of age and full maturity comes later. Even individual dogs within each breed have different healthcare requirements, so work with your veterinarian to determine what will be needed and what your role should be. This doctor-client relationship is important, because as vaccination guidelines change, there may not be an annual "vaccine visit" scheduled. You must make sure that you see your veterinarian at least annually, even if no vaccines are due, because this is the best opportunity to coordinate healthcare activities and to make sure that no medical issues creep by unaddressed.

When your Caucasian Mountain Dog reaches about eight years of age, he can be considered a "senior" and likely requires some special care. In general, if you've been taking great care of your canine companion throughout his formative and adult years, the transition to senior status should be a smooth one. Age is not a disease, and as long as everything is functioning as it should, there is no reason why most of late adulthood should not be rewarding for both you and your pet. This is especially true if you have tended to the details, such as regular veterinary visits, proper dental care, excellent nutrition and management of bone and joint issues.

At this stage in your Caucasian Mountain Dog's life, your veterinarian may want to schedule visits twice yearly, instead of once, to run some laboratory screenings, electrocardiograms and the like, and to change the diet to something more digestible. Catching problems early is the best way to manage them effectively. Treating the early stages of heart disease is so much easier than trying to intervene when there is more significant damage to the heart muscle. Similarly, managing the beginning of kidney problems is fairly routine if there is no significant kidney damage. Other problems, like cognitive dysfunction (similar to senility and Alzheimer's disease), cancer, diabetes and arthritis, are more common in older dogs, but all can be treated to help the dog live as many happy, comfortable years as possible. Just as in people, medical management is

WHAT IS "BLOAT" AND HOW DO I PREVENT IT?

You likely have heard the term "bloat," which refers to gastric torsion (gastric dilatation/volvulus), a potentially fatal condition. As any dog can be affected, a brief explanation here is warranted. The term *dilatation* means that the dog's stomach is filled with air, while *volvulus* means that the stomach is twisted around on itself, blocking the entrance/exit points. Dilatation/volvulus is truly a deadly combination, although they also can occur independently of each other. An affected dog cannot digest food or pass gas, and blood cannot flow to the stomach, causing accumulation of toxins and gas along with great pain and rapidly occurring shock.

Many theories exist on what exactly causes bloat, but we do know that large deep-chested breeds are more prone. Activities like eating a large meal, gulping water, strenuous exercise too close to mealtimes or a combination of these factors can contribute to bloat, though not every case is directly related to these more well-known causes. With that in mind, we can focus on incorporating simple daily preventives and knowing how to recognize the symptoms. In addition to the tips presented in this book, ask your vet about how to prevent and recognize bloat. An affected dog needs immediate veterinary attention, as death can result quickly. Signs include obvious restlessness/discomfort, crying in pain, drooling/excessive salivation, unproductive attempts to vomit or relieve himself, visibly bloated appearance and collapsing. Do not wait: get to the vet *right away* if you see any of these symptoms. The vet will confirm by x-ray if the stomach is bloated with air; if so, the dog must be treated *immediately*.

As varied as the causes of bloat are the tips for prevention, but some common preventive methods follow:
• Feed two or three small meals daily rather than one large one;
• Do not feed water before, after or with meals, but allow access to water at all other times;
• Never permit rapid eating or gulping of water;
• No exercise for the dog at least two hours before and (especially) after meals;
• Feed high-quality food with adequate protein, adequate fiber content and not too much fat and carbohydrate;
• Explore herbal additives, enzymes or gas-reduction products (only under a vet's advice) to encourage a "friendly" environment in the dog's digestive system;
• Avoid foods and ingredients known to produce gas;
• Avoid stressful situations for the dog, especially at mealtimes;
• Make dietary changes gradually, over a period of a few weeks;
• Do not feed dry food only;
• Although the role of genetics as a causative of bloat is not known, many breeders do not breed from previously affected dogs;
• Pay attention to your dog's behavior and any changes that could be symptomatic of bloat. Your dog's life depends on it!

more effective (and less expensive) when you catch things early.

SELECTING A VETERINARIAN

There is probably no more important decision that you will make regarding your pet's healthcare than the selection of his doctor. Your pet's veterinarian will be a pediatrician, family-practice physician and gerontologist, depending on the dog's life stage, and will be the individual who makes recommendations regarding issues such as when specialists need to be consulted, when diagnostic testing and/or therapeutic intervention is needed and when you will need to seek outside emergency and critical-care services. Your vet will act as

Part of good health is good grooming, especially in a breed as abundantly coated as the Caucasian Mountain Dog.

your advocate and liaison throughout these processes.

Everyone has his own idea about what to look for in a vet, an individual who will play a big role in his dog's (and, of course, his own) life for many years to come. For some, it is the compassionate caregiver with whom they hope to develop a professional relationship to span the lifetime of their dogs and even their future pets. For others, they are seeking a clinician with keen diagnostic and therapeutic insight who can deliver state-of-the-art healthcare. Still others need a veterinary facility that is open evenings and weekends, or is in close proximity or provides mobile veterinary services, to accommodate their schedules; these people may not much mind that their dogs might see different veterinarians on each visit. Just as we have different reasons for selecting our own healthcare professionals (e.g., covered by insurance plan, expert in field, convenient location, etc.), we should not expect that there is a one-size-fits-all recommendation for selecting a veterinarian and veterinary practice. The best advice is to be honest in your assessment of what you expect from a veterinary practice and to conscientiously research the options in your area. You will quickly appreciate that not all veterinary practices are the same, and you will be happiest with one that truly meets the needs of you and your Caucasian.

There is another point to be considered in the selection of veterinary services. Not that long ago, a single veterinarian would attempt to manage all medical and surgical issues as they arose. That was often problematic, because veterinarians are trained in many species and many diseases, and it was just impossible for general veterinary practitioners to be experts in every species, every field and every ailment. However, just as in the human healthcare fields, specialization has allowed general practitioners to concentrate on primary healthcare delivery, especially wellness and the prevention of infectious diseases, and to utilize a network of specialists to assist in the management of conditions that require specific expertise and experience. Thus there are now many types of veterinary specialists, including dermatologists, cardiologists, ophthalmologists, surgeons, internists, oncologists, neurologists, behaviorists, criticalists and others to help primary-care veterinarians deal with complicated medical challenges. In most cases, specialists see cases referred by primary-care veterinarians, make diagnoses and set up management plans. From there, the animals' ongoing care is returned to their primary-care veterinarians. This important team approach to your pet's medical-care needs has provided opportunities for advanced care and an unparalleled level of quality to be delivered.

YOUR DOG NEEDS TO VISIT THE VET IF:

- He has ingested a toxin such as antifreeze or a toxic plant; in these cases, administer first aid and call the vet right away
- His teeth are discolored, loose or missing or he has sores or other signs of infection or abnormality in the mouth
- He has been vomiting, has had diarrhea or has been constipated for over 24 hours; call immediately if you notice blood
- He has refused food for over 24 hours
- His eating habits, water intake or toilet habits have noticeably changed; if you have noticed weight gain or weight loss
- He shows symptoms of bloat, which requires *immediate* attention
- He is salivating excessively
- He has a lump in his throat
- He has a lump or bumps anywhere on the body
- He is very lethargic
- He appears to be in pain or otherwise has trouble chewing or swallowing
- His skin loses elasticity

Of course, there will be other instances in which a visit to the vet is necessary; these are just some of the signs that could be indicative of serious problems that need to be caught as early as possible.

Tiptoeing through the tulips might mean an itchy reaction for your dog! Dogs can be affected by many of the same allergens as people.

With all of the opportunities for your Caucasian Mountain Dog to receive high-quality veterinary medical care, there is another topic that needs to be addressed at the same time—cost. It's been said that you can have excellent healthcare or inexpensive healthcare, but never both; this is as true in veterinary medicine as it is in human medicine. While veterinary costs are a fraction of what the same services cost in the human health-care arena, it is still difficult to deal with unanticipated medical costs, especially since they can easily creep into hundreds or even thousands of dollars if specialists or emergency services become involved. However, there are ways of managing these risks. The easiest is to buy pet health insurance and realize that its foremost purpose is not to cover routine healthcare visits but rather to serve as an umbrella for those rainy days when your pet needs medical care and you don't want to worry about whether or not you can afford that care.

VACCINATIONS AND INFECTIOUS DISEASES

There has never been an easier time to prevent a variety of infectious diseases in your dog, but the advances we've made in veterinary medicine come with a price—choice. Now while it may seem that choice is a good thing (and it is), it has never been more

---

VETERINARY INSURANCE

Pet insurance policies are very cost-effective (and very inexpensive by human health-insurance standards), but make sure that you buy the policy long before you intend to use it (preferably starting in puppyhood, because coverage will exclude pre-existing conditions) and that you are actually buying an indemnity insurance plan from an insurance company that is regulated by your state or province. Many insurance policy look-alikes are actually discount clubs that are redeemable only at specific locations and for specific services. An indemnity plan covers your pet at almost all veterinary, specialty and emergency practices and is an excellent way to manage your pet's ongoing healthcare needs.

difficult for the pet owner (or the veterinarian) to make an informed decision about the best way to protect pets through vaccination.

Years ago, it was just accepted that puppies got a starter series of vaccinations and then annual "boosters" throughout their lives to keep them protected. As more and more vaccines became available, consumers wanted the convenience of having all of that protection in a single injection. The result was "multivalent" vaccines that crammed a lot of protection into a single syringe. The manufacturers' recommendations were to give the vaccines annually, and this was a simple enough protocol to follow. However, as veterinary medicine has become more sophisticated and we have started looking more at healthcare quandaries rather than convenience, it became necessary to reevaluate the situation and deal with some tough questions. It is important to realize that whether or not to use a particular vaccine depends on the risk of contracting the disease against which it protects, the severity of the disease if it is contracted, the duration of immunity provided by the vaccine, the safety of the product and the needs of the individual animal. In a very general sense, rabies, distemper, hepatitis and parvovirus are considered core vaccine needs, while parainfluenza, *Bordetella bronchiseptica*, leptospirosis, coronavirus

and borreliosis (Lyme disease) are considered non-core needs and best reserved for animals that demonstrate reasonable risk of contracting the diseases.

Pups start off with immunity conveyed by their mother's milk; their protection against disease is continued with vaccinations.

NEUTERING/SPAYING

Sterilization procedures (neutering for males/spaying for females) are meant to accomplish several purposes. While the underlying premise is to address the risk of pet overpopulation, there are also some medical and behavioral benefits to the surgeries as well. For females, spaying prior to the first estrus (heat cycle) leads to a marked reduction in the risk of mammary cancer. There also will be no manifestations of "heat" to attract male dogs and no bleeding in the house. For males, there is prevention of testicular cancer and a reduction in the risk of prostate problems. In both sexes, there may be some limited reduction in aggressive behaviors toward other dogs, and some diminishing of urine marking, roaming and mounting.

COMMON INFECTIOUS DISEASES

Let's discuss some of the diseases that create the need for vaccination in the first place. Following are the major canine infectious diseases and a simple explanation of each.

Rabies: A devastating viral disease that can be fatal in dogs and people. In fact, vaccination of dogs and cats is an important public-health measure to create a resistant animal buffer population to protect people from contracting the disease. Vaccination schedules are determined on a government level and are not optional for pet owners; rabies vaccination is required by law in all 50 states.

Parvovirus: A severe, potentially life-threatening disease that is easily transmitted between dogs. There are four strains of the virus, but it is believed that there is significant "cross-protection" between strains that may be included in individual vaccines.

Distemper: A potentially severe and life-threatening disease with a relatively high risk of exposure, especially in certain regions. In very high-risk distemper environments, young pups may be vaccinated with human measles vaccine, a related virus that offers cross-protection when administered at four to ten weeks of age.

Hepatitis: Caused by canine adenovirus type 1 (CAV-1), but since vaccination with the causative virus has a higher rate of adverse effects, cross-protection is derived from the use of adenovirus type 2 (CAV-2), a cause of respiratory disease and one of the potential causes of canine cough. Vaccination with CAV-2 provides long-term immunity against hepatitis, but relatively less protection against respiratory infection.

Canine cough: Also called tracheobronchitis, actually a fairly complicated result of viral and bacterial offenders; therefore, even with vaccination, protection is incomplete. Wherever dogs congregate, canine cough will likely be spread among them. Intranasal vaccination with *Bordetella* and parainfluenza is the best safeguard, but the duration of immunity does not appear to be very long, typically a year at most. These are non-core vaccines, but vaccination is sometimes mandated by boarding kennels, obedience classes, dog shows and other places where dogs congregate to try to minimize spread of infection.

Leptospirosis: A potentially fatal disease that is more common in some geographic regions. It is capable of being spread to humans. The disease varies with the individual "serovar," or strain, of *Leptospira* involved. Since there does not appear to be much cross-protection between serovars, protection is only as good as the likelihood that the serovar in the vaccine is the same as the one in the pet's local environment. Problems with *Leptospira* vaccines are that protection does not last very long, side effects are not uncommon and a large percentage of dogs (perhaps 30%) may not respond to vaccination.

Borrelia burgdorferi: The cause of Lyme disease, the risk of which varies with the geographic area in which the pet lives and travels. Lyme disease is spread by deer ticks in the eastern US and western black-legged ticks in the western part of the country, and the risk of exposure is high in some regions. Lameness, fever and inappetence are most commonly seen in affected dogs. The extent of protection from the vaccine has not been conclusively demonstrated.

Coronavirus: This disease has a high risk of exposure, especially in areas where dogs congregate, but it typically causes only mild to moderate digestive upset (diarrhea, vomiting, etc.). Vaccines are available, but the duration of protection is believed to be relatively short and the effectiveness of the vaccine in preventing infection is considered low.

There are many other vaccinations available, including those for *Giardia* and canine adenovirus-1. While there may be some specific indications for their use, and local risk factors to be considered, they are not widely recommended for most dogs.

While neutering and spaying do indeed prevent animals from contributing to pet overpopulation, even no-cost and low-cost neutering options have not eliminated the problem. Perhaps one of the main reasons for this is that individuals that intentionally breed their dogs and those that allow their animals to run at large are the main causes of unwanted offspring. Also, animals in shelters are often there because they were abandoned or relinquished, not because they came from unplanned matings. Neutering/spaying is important, but it should be considered in the context of the real causes of animals' ending up in shelters and eventually being euthanized.

One of the important considerations regarding neutering is that it is a surgical procedure. This sometimes gets lost in discussions of low-cost procedures and commoditization of the process. In females, spaying is specifically referred to as an ovariohysterectomy. In this procedure, a midline incision is made in the abdomen and the entire uterus and both ovaries are surgically removed. While this is a major invasive surgical procedure, it usually has few complications, because it is typically performed on healthy young animals. However, it is major surgery, as any woman who has had a hysterectomy will attest.

In males, neutering has traditionally referred to castration, which involves the surgical removal of both testicles. While still a significant piece of surgery, there is not the abdominal exposure that is required in the female surgery. In addition, there is now a chemical sterilization option, in which a solution is injected into each testicle, leading to atrophy of the sperm-producing cells. This can typically be done under sedation rather than full anesthesia. This is a relatively new approach, and there are no long-term clinical studies yet available.

Neutering/spaying is typically done around six months of age at most veterinary hospitals, although techniques have been pioneered to perform the procedures in animals as young as eight weeks of age. In general, the surgeries on the very young animals are done for the specific reason of sterilizing them before they go to their new homes. This is done in some shelter hospitals for assurance that the animals will definitely not produce any pups. Otherwise, these organizations need to rely on owners to comply with their wishes to have the animals "altered" at a later date, something that does not always happen. Breeders usually require in their contracts that owners of pet pups, not of sufficient quality for breeding, have their pups spayed/neutered at the appropriate age.

S. E. M. by Dr. Dennis Kunkel, University of Hawaii

A scanning electron micrograph of a dog flea, Ctenocephalides canis, on dog hair.

EXTERNAL PARASITES

FLEAS

Fleas have been around for millions of years and, while we have better tools now for controlling them than at any time in the past, there still is little chance that they will end up on an endangered species list. Actually, they are very well adapted to living on our pets, and they continue to adapt as we make advances.

The female flea can consume 15 times her weight in blood during active reproduction and can lay as many as 40 eggs a day. These eggs are very resistant to the effects of insecticides. They hatch into larvae, which then mature and spin cocoons. The immature fleas reside in this pupal stage until the time is right for feeding. This pupal stage is also very resistant to the effects of insecticides, and pupae can last in the environment without feeding for many months. Newly emergent fleas are attracted to animals by the warmth of the animals' bodies, movement and exhaled carbon dioxide. However, when they first emerge from their cocoons, they orient towards light; thus when an animal passes between a flea and the light source, casting a shadow, the flea pounces and starts to feed. If the animal turns out to be a dog or cat, the reproductive cycle continues. If the flea lands on another type of animal, including a person, the flea will bite but will then look for a more appropriate host. An emerging adult flea can survive without feeding for up to 12 months but, once it tastes blood, it can survive off its host for only three to four days.

It was once thought that fleas spend most of their lives in the environment, but we now know that fleas won't willingly jump off a dog unless leaping to another dog or when physically removed by brushing, bathing or other manipulation. Flea eggs, on the other hand, are shiny and smooth, and they roll off the animal and into the environment. The eggs, larvae and pupae then exist in the environment, but once the adult finds a susceptible animal, it's home sweet home until the flea is forced to seek refuge elsewhere.

Since adult fleas live on the animal and immature forms survive in the environment, a successful treatment plan must address all stages of the flea life cycle. There are now several safe and effective flea-control products that can be applied on a monthly

> **FLEA PREVENTION FOR YOUR DOG**
> - Discuss with your veterinarian the safest product to protect your dog, likely in the form of a monthly tablet or a liquid preparation placed on the back of the dog's neck.
> - For dogs suffering from flea-bite dermatitis, a shampoo or topical insecticide treatment is required.
> - Your lawn and property should be sprayed with an insecticide designed to kill fleas and ticks that lurk outdoors.
> - Using a flea comb, check the dog's coat regularly for any signs of parasites.
> - Practice good housekeeping. Vacuum floors, carpets and furniture regularly, especially in the areas that the dog frequents, and wash the dog's bedding weekly.
> - Follow up house-cleaning with carpet shampoos and sprays to rid the house of fleas at all stages of development. Insect growth regulators are the safest option.

basis. These include fipronil, imidacloprid, selamectin and permethrin (found in several formulations). Most of these products have significant flea-killing rates within 24 hours. However, none of them will control the immature forms in the environment. To accomplish this, there are a variety of insect growth regulators that can be sprayed into

THE FLEA'S LIFE CYCLE

What came first, the flea or the egg? This age-old mystery is more difficult to comprehend than the actual cycle of the flea. Fleas usually live only about four months. A female can lay 2,000 eggs in her lifetime.

Egg

After ten days of rolling around your carpet or under your furniture, the eggs hatch into larvae, which feed on various and sundry debris. In days or months, depending on the climate, the larvae spin cocoons and develop into the pupal or nymph stage, which quickly develop into fleas.

Larva

Pupa

These immature fleas must locate a host within 10 to 14 days or they will die. Only about 1% of the flea population exist as adult fleas, while the other 99% exist as eggs, larvae or pupae.

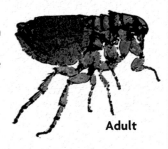

Adult

Photo by Carolina Biological Supply Co.

KILL FLEAS THE NATURAL WAY

If you choose not to go the route of conventional medication, there are some natural ways to ward off fleas:

• Dust your dog with a natural flea powder, composed of such herbal goodies as rosemary, wormwood, pennyroyal, citronella, rue, tobacco powder and eucalyptus.

• Apply diatomaceous earth, the fossilized remains of single-cell algae, to your carpets, furniture and pet's bedding. Even though it's not good for dogs, it's even worse for fleas, which will dry up swiftly and die.

• Brush your dog frequently, give him adequate exercise and let him fast occasionally. All of these activities strengthen the dog's system and make him more resistant to disease and parasites.

• Bathe your dog with a capful of pennyroyal or eucalyptus oil.

• Feed a natural diet, free of additives and preservatives. Add some fresh garlic and brewer's yeast to the dog's morning portion, as these items have flea-repelling properties.

the environment (e.g., pyriprox-yfen, methoprene, fenoxycarb) as well as insect development inhibitors such as lufenuron that can be administered. These compounds have no effect on adult fleas, but they stop imma-ture forms from developing into adults. In years gone by, we relied heavily on toxic insecticides (such as organophosphates, organochlo-rines and carbamates) to manage the flea problem, but today's options are not only much safer to use on our pets but also safer for the environment.

TICKS

Ticks are members of the spider class (arachnids) and are blood-sucking parasites capable of transmitting a variety of diseases, including Lyme disease, ehrlichiosis, babesiosis and Rocky Mountain spotted fever. It's easy to see ticks on your own skin, but it is more of a challenge when your furry companion is affected. Whenever you happen to be planning a stroll in a tick-infested area (especially forests, grassy or wooded areas or parks) be prepared to do a thorough inspection of your dog afterward to search for ticks. Ticks can be tricky, so make sure you spend time looking in the ears, between the toes and everywhere else where a tick might hide. Ticks need to be attached for 24–72 hours before they transmit most of the diseases that they carry, so you do have a window of opportunity for some preventive intervention.

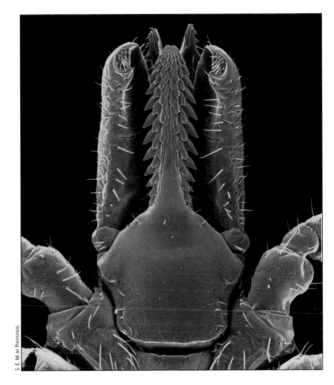

A scanning electron micrograph of the head of a female deer tick, *Ixodes dammini*, a parasitic tick that carries Lyme disease.

A TICKING BOMB

There is nothing good about a tick's harpooning his nose into your dog's skin. Among the diseases caused by ticks are Rocky Mountain spotted fever, canine ehrlichiosis, canine babesiosis, canine hepatozoonosis and Lyme disease. If a dog is allergic to the saliva of a female wood tick, he can develop tick paralysis.

Female ticks live to eat and breed. They can lay between 4,000 and 5,000 eggs and they die soon after. Males, on the other hand, live only to mate with the females and continue the process as long as they are able. Most ticks live on multiple hosts before parasitizing dogs. The immature forms typically reside on grass and shrubs, waiting for susceptible animals to walk by. The larvae and nymph stages typically feed on wildlife.

If only a few ticks are present on a dog, they can be plucked out, but it is important to remove the entire head and mouthparts,

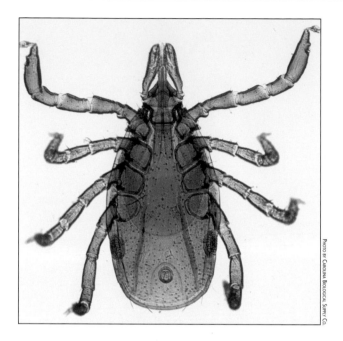

**Deer tick,
Ixodes dammini.**

PHOTO BY CAROLINA BIOLOGICAL SUPPLY CO.

of in a container of alcohol or household bleach.

Some of the newer flea products, specifically those with fipronil, selamectin and permethrin, have effect against some, but not all, species of tick. Flea collars containing appropriate pesticides (e.g., propoxur, chlorfenvinphos) can aid in tick control. In most areas, such collars should be placed on animals in March, at the beginning of the tick season, and changed regularly. Leaving the collar on when the pesticide level is waning invites the development of resistance. Amitraz collars are also good for tick control, and the active ingredient does not interfere with other flea-control products. The ingredient helps prevent the attachment of ticks to the skin and will cause those ticks already on the skin to detach themselves.

which may be deeply embedded in the skin. This is best accomplished with forceps designed especially for this purpose; fingers can be used but should be protected with rubber gloves, plastic wrap or at least a paper towel. The tick should be grasped as closely as possible to the animal's skin and should be pulled upward with steady, even pressure. Do not squeeze, crush or puncture the body of the tick or you risk exposure to any disease carried by that tick. Once the ticks have been removed, the sites of attachment should be disinfected. Your hands should then be washed with soap and water to further minimize risk of contagion. The tick should be disposed

TICK CONTROL

Removal of underbrush and leaf litter and the thinning of trees in areas where tick control is desired are recommended. These actions remove the cover and food sources for small animals that serve as hosts for ticks. With continued mowing of grasses in these areas, the probability of ticks' surviving is further reduced. A variety of insecticide ingredients (e.g., resmethrin, carbaryl, permethrin, chlorpyrifos, dioxathion and allethrin) are registered for tick control around the home.

MITES

Mites are tiny arachnid parasites that parasitize the skin of dogs. Skin diseases caused by mites are referred to as "mange," and there are many different forms seen in dogs. These forms are very different from one another, each one warranting an individual description.

Sarcoptic mange, or scabies, is one of the itchiest conditions that affects dogs. The microscopic *Sarcoptes* mites burrow into the superficial layers of the skin and can drive dogs crazy with itchiness. They are also communicable to people, although they can't complete their reproductive cycle on people. In addition to being tiny, the mites also are often difficult to find when trying to make a diagnosis. Skin scrapings from multiple areas are examined microscopically but, even then, sometimes the mites cannot be found.

Fortunately, scabies is relatively easy to treat, and there are a variety of products that will successfully kill the mites. Since the mites can't live in the environment for very long without feeding, a complete cure is usually possible within four to eight weeks.

Cheyletiellosis is caused by a relatively large mite, which sometimes can be seen even without a microscope. Often referred to as "walking dandruff," this also causes itching, but not usually as profound as with scabies. While *Cheyletiella* mites can survive somewhat longer

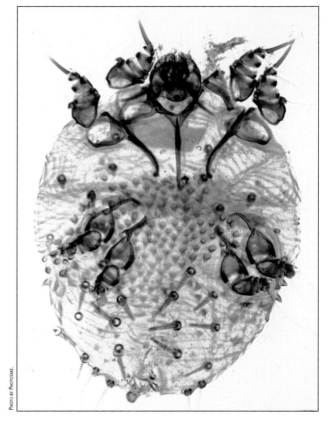

PHOTO BY PHOTOTAKE.

Sarcoptes scabiei, commonly known as the "itch mite."

in the environment than scabies mites, they too are relatively easy to treat, being responsive to not only the medications used to treat scabies but also often to flea-control products.

Otodectes cynotis is the canine ear mite and is one of the more common causes of mange, especially in young dogs in shelters or pet stores. That's because the mites are typically present in large numbers and are quickly spread to nearby animals. The mites rarely do much harm but can be difficult

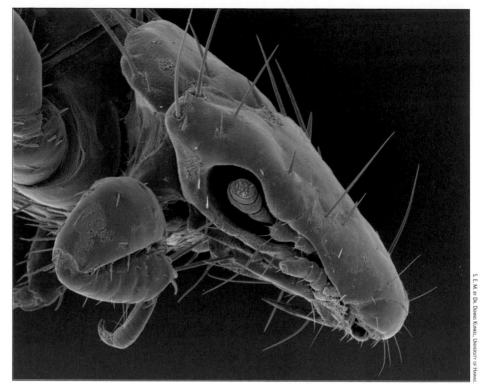

Micrograph of a dog louse, *Heterodoxus spiniger*. Female lice attach their eggs to the hairs of the dog. As the eggs hatch, the larval lice bite and feed on the blood. Lice can also feed on dead skin and hair. This feeding activity can cause hair loss and skin problems.

S. E. M. BY DR. DENNIS KUNKEL, UNIVERSITY OF HAWAII.

to eradicate if the treatment regimen is not comprehensive. While many try to treat the condition with ear drops only, this is the most common cause of treatment failure. Ear drops cause the mites to simply move out of the ears and as far away as possible (usually to the base of the tail) until the insecticide levels in the ears drop to an acceptable level—then it's back to business as usual! The successful treatment of ear mites requires treating all animals in the household with a systemic insecticide, such as selamectin, or a combination of miticidal ear drops

combined with whole-body flea-control preparations.

Demodicosis, sometimes referred to as red mange, can be one of the most difficult forms of mange to treat. Part of the problem has to do with the fact that the mites live in the hair follicles and they are relatively well shielded from topical and systemic products. The main issue, however, is that demodectic mange typically results only when there is some underlying process interfering with the dog's immune system.

Since *Demodex* mites are normal residents of the skin of

mammals, including humans, there is usually a mite population explosion only when the immune system fails to keep the number of mites in check. In young animals, the immune deficit may be transient or may reflect an actual inherited immune problem. In older animals, demodicosis is usually seen only when there is another disease hampering the immune system, such as diabetes, cancer, thyroid problems or the use of immune-suppressing drugs. Accordingly, treatment involves not only trying to kill the mange mites but also discerning what is interfering with immune function and correcting it if possible.

Chiggers represent several different species of mite that don't parasitize dogs specifically, but do latch on to passersby and can cause irritation. The problem is most prevalent in wooded areas in the late summer and fall. Treatment is not difficult, as the mites do not complete their life cycle on dogs and are susceptible to a variety of miticidal products.

MOSQUITOES

Mosquitoes have long been known to transmit a variety of diseases to people, as well as just being biting pests during warm weather. They also pose a real risk to pets. Not only do they carry deadly heartworms but

ILLUSTRATION BY PhototakE

Illustration of Demodex folliculoram.

recently there also has been much concern over their involvement with West Nile virus. While we can avoid heartworm with the use of preventive medications, there are no such preventives for West Nile virus. The only method of prevention in endemic areas is active mosquito control. Fortunately, most dogs that have been exposed to the virus only developed flu-like symptoms and, to date, there have not been the large number of reported deaths in canines as seen in some other species.

MOSQUITO REPELLENT

Low concentrations of DEET (less than 10%), found in many human mosquito repellents, have been safely used in dogs but, in these concentrations, probably give only about two hours of protection. DEET may be safe in these small concentrations, but since it is not licensed for use on dogs, there is no research proving its safety for dogs. Products containing permethrin give the longest-lasting protection, perhaps two to four weeks. As DEET is not licensed for use on dogs, and both DEET and permethrin can be quite toxic to cats, appropriate care should be exercised. Other products, such as those containing oil of citronella, also have some mosquito-repellent activity, but typically have a relatively short duration of action.

ASCARID DANGERS

The most commonly encountered worms in dogs are roundworms known as ascarids. *Toxascaris leonine* and *Toxocara canis* are the two species that infect dogs. Subsisting in the dog's stomach and intestines, adult round-worms can grow to 7 inches in length and adult females can lay in excess of 200,000 eggs in a single day.

In humans, visceral larval migrans affects people who have ingested eggs of *Toxocara canis*, which frequently contaminates children's sandboxes, beaches and park grounds. The round-worms reside in the human's stomach and intestines, as they would in a dog's, but do not mature. Instead, they find their way to the liver, lungs and skin, or even to the heart or kidneys in severe cases. Deworming puppies is critical in preventing the infection in humans, and young children should never handle nursing pups who have not been dewormed.

The ascarid roundworm *Toxocara canis*, showing the mouth with three lips. INSET: Photomicrograph of the roundworm *Ascaris lumbricoides*.

INTERNAL PARASITES: WORMS

ASCARIDS

Ascarids are intestinal round-worms that rarely cause severe disease in dogs. Nonetheless, they are of major public health significance because they can be transferred to people. Sadly, it is children who are most commonly affected by the parasite, probably from inadvertently ingesting ascarid-contaminated soil. In fact, many yards and children's sand-boxes contain appreciable numbers of ascarid eggs. So, while ascarids don't bite dogs or latch onto their intestines to suck blood, they do cause some nasty medical conditions in children and are best eradicated from our furry friends. Because pups can start passing ascarid eggs by three weeks of age, most parasite-control programs begin at two weeks of age and are repeated every two weeks until pups are eight weeks old. It is important to

HOOKED ON ANCYLOSTOMA

Adult dogs can become infected by the bloodsucking nematodes we commonly call hookworms via ingesting larvae from the ground or via the larvae penetrating the dog's skin. It is not uncommon for infected dogs to show no symptoms of hookworm infestation. Sometimes symptoms occur within ten days of exposure. These symptoms can include bloody diarrhea, anemia, loss of weight and general weakness. Dogs pass the hookworm eggs in their stools, which serves as the vet's method of identifying the infestation. The hookworm larvae can encyst themselves in the dog's tissues and be released when the dog is experiencing stress.

Caused by an *Ancylostoma* species whose common host is the dog, cutaneous larval migrans affects humans, causing itching and lumps and streaks beneath the surface of the skin.

S. E. M. BY DR. DENNIS KUNKEL, UNIVERSITY OF HAWAII.

realize that bitches can pass ascarids to their pups even if they test negative prior to whelping. Accordingly, bitches are best treated at the same time as the pups.

HOOKWORMS

Unlike ascarids, hookworms do latch onto a dog's intestinal tract and can cause significant loss of blood and protein. Similar to ascarids, hookworms can be transmitted to humans, where they cause a condition known as cutaneous larval migrans. Dogs can become infected either by consuming the infective larvae or by the larvae's penetrating the skin directly. People most often get infected when they are lying on the ground (such as on a beach) and the larvae penetrate the skin. Yes, the larvae can penetrate through a beach blanket. Hookworms are typically susceptible to the same medications used to treat ascarids.

The hookworm *Ancylostoma caninum* infests the intestines of dogs. INSET: Note the row of hooks at the posterior end, used to anchor the worm to the intestinal wall.

WHIPWORMS

Whipworms latch onto the lower aspects of the dog's colon and can cause cramping and diarrhea. Eggs do not start to appear in the dog's feces until about three months after the dog was infected. This worm has a peculiar life cycle, which makes it more difficult to control than ascarids or hookworms. The good thing is that whipworms rarely are transferred to people.

Some of the medications used to treat ascarids and hookworms are also effective against whipworms, but, in general, a separate treatment protocol is needed. Since most of the medications are effective against the adults but not the eggs or larvae, treatment is typically repeated in three weeks, and then often in three

Adult whipworm, *Trichuris* sp., an intestinal parasite.

S. E. M. BY DR. DENNIS KUNKEL, UNIVERSITY OF HAWAII

WORM-CONTROL GUIDELINES

- Practice sanitary habits with your dog and home.
- Clean up after your dog and don't let him sniff or eat other dogs' droppings.
- Control insects and fleas in the dog's environment. Fleas, lice, cockroaches, beetles, mice and rats can act as hosts for various worms.
- Prevent dogs from eating uncooked meat, raw poultry and dead animals.
- Keep dogs and children from playing in sand and soil.
- Kennel dogs on cement or gravel; avoid dirt runs.
- Administer heartworm preventives regularly.
- Have your vet examine your dog's stools at your annual visits.
- Select a boarding kennel carefully so as to avoid contamination from other dogs or an unsanitary environment.
- Prevent dogs from roaming. Obey local leash laws.

months as well. Unfortunately, since dogs don't develop resistance to whipworms, it is difficult to prevent them from getting reinfected if they visit soil contaminated with whipworm eggs.

TAPEWORMS

There are many different species of tapeworm that affect dogs, but *Dipylidium caninum* is probably the most common and is spread by fleas. Flea larvae feed on organic debris and tapeworm eggs in the environment and, when a dog chews at himself and manages to ingest fleas, he might get a dose of tapeworm at the same time. The tapeworm then develops further in the intestine of the dog.

The tapeworm itself, which is a parasitic flatworm that latches onto the intestinal wall, is composed of numerous segments. When the segments break off into the intestine (as proglottids), they may accumulate around the rectum, like grains of rice. While this tapeworm is disgusting in its behavior, it is not directly communicable to humans (although humans can also get infected by swallowing fleas).

A much more dangerous flatworm is *Echinococcus multilocularis*, which is typically found in foxes, coyotes and wolves. The eggs are passed in the feces and infect rodents, and, when dogs eat the rodents, the dogs can be infected by thousands of adult tapeworms. While the parasites don't cause many problems in dogs, this is considered the most lethal worm infection that people can get. Take appropriate precautions if you live in an area in which these tapeworms are found. Do not use mulch that may contain feces of dogs, cats or wildlife, and discourage your pets from hunting

wildlife. Treat these tapeworm infections aggressively in pets, because if humans get infected, approximately half die.

HEARTWORMS

Heartworm disease is caused by the parasite *Dirofilaria immitis* and is seen in dogs around the world. A member of the roundworm group, it is spread between dogs by the bite of an infected mosquito. The mosquito injects infective larvae into the dog's skin with its bite, and these larvae develop under the skin for a period of time before making their way to the heart. There they develop into adults, which grow and create blockages of the heart, lungs and major blood vessels. They also start producing offspring (microfilariae)

A dog tapeworm proglottid (body segment).

The dog tapeworm *Taenia pisiformis.*

S. E. M. BY DR. DENNIS KUNKEL, UNIVERSITY OF HAWAII.

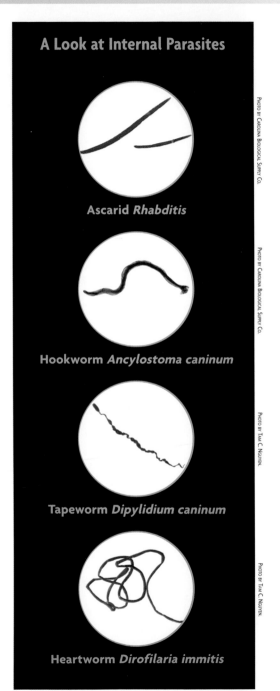

A Look at Internal Parasites

Ascarid *Rhabditis*

Hookworm *Ancylostoma caninum*

Tapeworm *Dipylidium caninum*

Heartworm *Dirofilaria immitis*

PHOTO BY CAROLINA BIOLOGICAL SUPPLY CO.

PHOTO BY CAROLINA BIOLOGICAL SUPPLY CO.

PHOTO BY TAM C. NGUYEN

PHOTO BY TAM C. NGUYEN

and these microfilariae circulate in the bloodstream, waiting to hitch a ride when the next mosquito bites. Once in the mosquito, the microfilariae develop into infective larvae and the entire process is repeated.

When dogs get infected with heartworm, over time they tend to develop symptoms associated with heart disease, such as coughing, exercise intolerance and potentially many other manifestations. Diagnosis is confirmed by either seeing the microfilariae themselves in blood samples or using immunologic tests (antigen testing) to identify the presence of adult heartworms. Since antigen tests measure the presence of adult heartworms and microfilarial tests measure offspring produced by adults, neither are positive until six to seven months after the initial infection. However, the beginning of damage can occur by fifth-stage larvae as early as three months after infection. Thus it is possible for dogs to be harboring problem-causing larvae for up to three months before either type of test would identify an infection.

The good news is that there are great protocols available for preventing heartworm in dogs. Testing is critical in the process, and it is important to understand the benefits as well as the limitations of such testing. All dogs six months of age or older that have not been on continuous heartworm-preventive medication

Life Cycle of the Heartworm

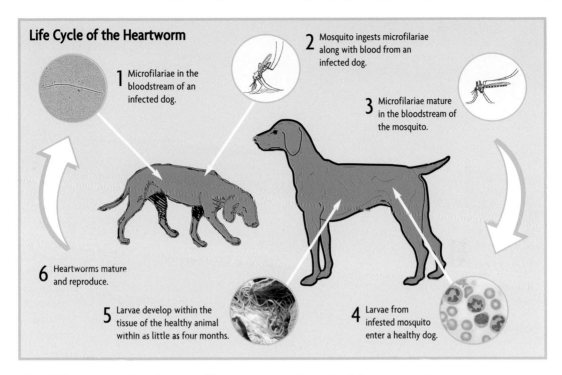

1 Microfilariae in the bloodstream of an infected dog.

2 Mosquito ingests microfilariae along with blood from an infected dog.

3 Microfilariae mature in the bloodstream of the mosquito.

4 Larvae from infested mosquito enter a healthy dog.

5 Larvae develop within the tissue of the healthy animal within as little as four months.

6 Heartworms mature and reproduce.

should be screened with microfilarial or antigen tests. For dogs receiving preventive medication, periodic antigen testing helps assess the effectiveness of the preventives. The American Heartworm Society guidelines suggest that annual retesting may not be necessary when owners have absolutely provided continuous heartworm prevention. Retesting on a two- to three-year interval may be sufficient in these cases. However, your veterinarian will likely have specific guidelines under which heartworm preventives will be prescribed, and many prefer to err on the side of safety and retest annually.

It is indeed fortunate that heartworm is relatively easy to prevent, because treatments can be as life-threatening as the disease itself. Treatment requires a two-step process that kills the adult heartworms first and then the microfilariae. Prevention is obviously preferable; this involves a once-monthly oral or topical treatment. The most common oral preventives include ivermectin (not suitable for some breeds), moxidectin and milbemycin oxime; the once-a-month topical drug selamectin provides heartworm protection in addition to flea, tick and other parasite controls.

THE **ABC**s OF
Emergency Care

Abrasions
Clean wound with running water or 3% hydrogen peroxide. Pat dry with gauze and spray with antibiotic. Do not cover.

Animal Bites
Clean area with soap and saline solution or water. Apply pressure to any bleeding area. Apply antibiotic ointment.

Antifreeze Poisoning
Induce vomiting and take dog to the vet.

Bee Sting
Remove stinger and apply soothing lotion or cold compress; give antihistamine in proper dosage.

Bleeding
Apply pressure directly to wound with gauze or towel for five to ten minutes. If wound does not stop bleeding, wrap wound with gauze and adhesive tape.

Bloat/Gastric Torsion
Immediately take the dog to the vet or emergency clinic; phone from car. No time to waste.

Burns
Chemical: Bathe dog with water and pet shampoo. Rinse in saline solution. Apply antibiotic ointment.

Acid: Rinse with water. Apply one part baking soda, two parts water to affected area.

Alkali: Rinse with water. Apply one part vinegar, four parts water to affected area.

Electrical: Apply antibiotic ointment. Seek veterinary assistance immediately.

Choking
If the dog is on the verge of collapsing, wedge a solid object, such as the handle of screwdriver, between molars on one side of mouth to keep mouth open. Pull tongue out. Use long-nosed pliers or fingers to remove foreign object. Do not push the object down the dog's throat. For small or medium dogs, hold dog upside down by hind legs and shake firmly to dislodge foreign object.

Chlorine Ingestion
With clean water, rinse the mouth and eyes. Give dog water to drink; contact the vet.

Constipation
Feed dog 2 tablespoons bran flakes with each meal. Encourage drinking water. Mix 1/4 teaspoon mineral oil in dog's food.

Diarrhea
Withhold food for 12 to 24 hours. Feed dog anti-diarrheal with eyedropper. When feeding resumes, feed one part boiled hamburger, one part plain cooked rice, 1/4 to 3/4 cup four times daily.

Dog Bite
Snip away hair around puncture wound; clean with 3% hydrogen peroxide; apply tincture of iodine. If wound appears deep, take the dog to the vet.

Frostbite
Wrap the dog in a heavy blanket. Warm affected area with a warm bath for ten minutes. Red color to skin will return with circulation; if tissues are pale after 20 minutes, contact the vet.

Use a portable, durable container large enough to contain all items

Heat Stroke
Submerge the dog in cold water; if no response within ten minutes, contact the vet.

Hot Spots
Mix 2 packets Domeboro® with 2 cups water. Saturate cloth with mixture and apply to hot spots for 15–30 minutes. Apply antibiotic ointment. Repeat every six to eight hours.

Poisonous Plants
Wash affected area with soap and water. Cleanse with alcohol. For foxtail/grass, apply antibiotic ointment.

Rat Poison Ingestion
Induce vomiting. Keep dog calm, maintain dog's normal body temperature (use blanket or heating pad). Get to the vet for antidote.

Shock
Keep the dog calm and warm; call for veterinary assistance.

Snake Bite
If possible, bandage the area and apply pressure. If the area is not conducive to bandaging, use ice to control bleeding. Get immediate help from the vet.

Tick Removal
Apply flea and tick spray directly on tick. Wait one minute. Using tweezers or wearing plastic gloves, grasp the tick's body firmly. Apply antibiotic ointment.

Vomiting
Restrict dog's water intake; offer a few ice cubes. Withhold food for next meal. Contact vet if vomiting persists longer than 24 hours.

DOG OWNER'S FIRST-AID KIT
❑ **Gauze bandages/swabs**
❑ **Adhesive and non-adhesive bandages**
❑ **Antibiotic powder**
❑ **Antiseptic wash**
❑ **Hydrogen peroxide 3%**
❑ **Antibiotic ointment**
❑ **Lubricating jelly**
❑ **Rectal thermometer**
❑ **Nylon muzzle**
❑ **Scissors and forceps**
❑ **Eyedropper**
❑ **Syringe**
❑ **Anti-bacterial/fungal solution**
❑ **Saline solution**
❑ **Antihistamine**
❑ **Cotton balls**
❑ **Nail clippers**
❑ **Screwdriver/pen knife**
❑ **Flashlight**
❑ **Emergency phone numbers**

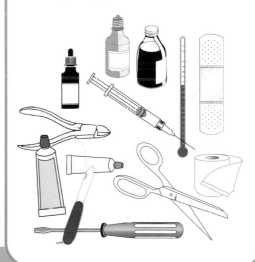

Number-One Killer Disease in Dogs: CANCER

In every age, there is a word associated with a disease or plague that causes humans to shudder. In the 21st century, that word is "cancer." Just as cancer is the leading cause of death in humans, it claims nearly half the lives of dogs that die from a natural disease as well as half the dogs that die over the age of ten years.

Described as a genetic disease, cancer becomes a greater risk as the dog ages. Vets and dog owners have become increasingly aware of the threat of cancer to dogs. Statistics reveal that one dog in every five will develop cancer, the most common of which is skin cancer. Many cancers, including prostate, ovarian and breast cancer, can be avoided by spaying and neutering our dogs by the age of six months.

Early detection of cancer can save or extend a dog's life, so it is absolutely vital for owners to have their dogs examined by a qualified vet or oncologist immediately upon detection of any abnormality. Certain dietary guidelines have also proven to reduce the onset and spread of cancer. Foods based on fish rather than beef, due to the presence of Omega-3 fatty acids, are recommended. Other amino acids such as glutamine have significant benefits for canines, particularly those breeds that show a greater susceptibility to cancer.

Cancer management and treatments promise hope for future generations of canines. Since the disease is genetic, breeders should never breed a dog whose parents, grandparents and any related siblings have developed cancer. It is difficult to know whether to exclude an otherwise healthy dog from a breeding program, as the disease does not manifest itself until the dog's senior years.

RECOGNIZE CANCER WARNING SIGNS

Since early detection can possibly rescue your dog from becoming a cancer statistic, it is essential for owners to recognize the possible signs and seek the assistance of a qualified professional.

- Abnormal bumps or lumps that continue to grow
- Bleeding or discharge from any body cavity
- Persistent stiffness or lameness
- Recurrent sores or sores that do not heal
- Inappetence
- Breathing difficulties
- Weight loss
- Bad breath or odors
- General malaise and fatigue
- Eating and swallowing problems
- Difficulty urinating and defecating

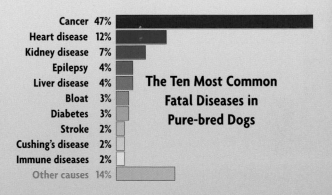

Disease	%
Cancer	47%
Heart disease	12%
Kidney disease	7%
Epilepsy	4%
Liver disease	4%
Bloat	3%
Diabetes	3%
Stroke	2%
Cushing's disease	2%
Immune diseases	2%
Other causes	14%

The Ten Most Common Fatal Diseases in Pure-bred Dogs

COGNITIVE DYSFUNCTION SYNDROME

"OLD-DOG SYNDROME"

There are many ways for you to evaluate old-dog syndrome. Veterinarians have defined cognitive dysfunction syndrome as the gradual deterioration of cognitive abilities, indicated by changes in the dog's behavior. When a dog changes his routine response, and maladies have been eliminated as the cause of these behavioral changes, then CDS is the usual diagnosis.

More than half the dogs over eight years old suffer from some form of CDS. The older the dog, the more chance he has of suffering from CDS. In humans, doctors often dismiss the CDS behavioral changes as part of "winding down."

There are four major signs of CDS: frequent potty accidents inside the home, sleeping much more or much less than normal, acting confused and failing to respond to social stimuli.

SYMPTOMS OF CDS

FREQUENT POTTY ACCIDENTS
- Urinates in the house.
- Defecates in the house.
- Doesn't signal that he wants to go out.

FAILURE TO RESPOND TO SOCIAL STIMULI
- Comes to people less frequently, whether called or not.
- Doesn't tolerate petting for more than a short time.
- Doesn't come to the door when you return home.

CONFUSION
- Goes outside and just stands there.
- Appears confused with a faraway look in his eyes.
- Hides more often.
- Doesn't recognize friends.
- Doesn't come when called.
- Walks around listlessly and without a destination.

SLEEP PATTERNS
- Awakens more slowly.
- Sleeps more than normal during the day.
- Sleeps less during the night.

SHOWING YOUR
CAUCASIAN MOUNTAIN DOG

Is dog showing in your blood? Are you excited by the idea of gaiting your handsome Caucasian Mountain Dog around the ring to the thunderous applause of an enthusiastic audience? Are you certain that your beloved Caucasian Mountain Dog is flawless? You are not alone! Every loving owner thinks that his dog has no faults, or too few to mention. No matter how many times an owner reads the

breed standard, he cannot find any faults in his aristocratic companion dog. If this sounds like you, and if you are considering entering your Caucasian Mountain Dog in a dog show, here are some basic questions to ask yourself:

- Did you purchase a "show-quality" puppy from the breeder?
- Is your puppy at least six months of age?
- Does the puppy exhibit correct show type for his breed?
- Does your puppy have any disqualifying faults?
- Is your Caucasian Mountain Dog registered with the hosting kennel club?
- How much time do you have to devote to training, grooming, conditioning and exhibiting your dog?
- Do you understand the rules and regulations of a dog show?
- Do you have time to learn how to show your dog properly?
- Do you have the financial resources to invest in showing your dog?
- Do you have a vehicle that can accommodate your weekend trips to the dog shows?

SHOW POTENTIAL

How possible is it to predict how your ten-week-old puppy will eventually do in the show ring? Most show dogs reach their prime at around three years of age, when their bodies are physically mature and their coats are in "full bloom." Experienced breeders, having watched countless pups grow into Best of Breed winners, recognize the glowing attributes that spell "show potential." When selecting a puppy for show, it's best to trust the breeder to recommend which puppy will best suit your aspirations. Some breeders recommend starting with a male puppy, which likely will be more "typey" than his female counterpart.

Success in the show ring requires more than a pretty face, a waggy tail and a pocketful of liver. Even though dog shows can be exciting and enjoyable, the sport of conformation makes great demands on the exhibitors and the dogs. Winning exhibitors live for their dogs, devoting time and money to their dogs' presentation, conditioning and training. Very few novices, even those with good dogs, will find themselves in the winners' circle, though it does happen. Don't be disheartened, though. Every exhibitor began as a novice and worked his way up to the group ring. It's the "working your way up" part that you must keep in mind.

Assuming that you have purchased a puppy of the correct type and quality for showing, let's begin to examine the world of showing and what's required to get started. Although the entry fee into a dog show is nominal, there are lots of other hidden costs involved with "finishing" your Caucasian Mountain Dog, that is, making him a champion. Things like equipment, travel, training and conditioning all cost money. A more serious campaign will include fees for a professional handler, boarding, cross-country travel and advertising. Top-winning show dogs can represent a very considerable investment— over $100,000 has been spent in campaigning some dogs. (The

investment can be less, of course, for owners who don't use professional handlers.)

Many owners, on the other hand, enter their "average" Caucasian Mountain Dogs in dog shows for the fun and enjoyment of it. Dog showing makes an absorbing hobby, with many rewards for dogs and owners alike. If you're having fun, meeting other people who share your interests and enjoying the overall experience, you likely will catch the "bug." Once the dog-show bug bites, its effects can last a lifetime; it's certainly much better than a deer tick! Soon you will be envisioning yourself in the center ring, competing for Best in Show.

A handsome Caucasian Mountain Dog pictured at a show in the UK.

RARE-BREED SHOWING

THE UNITED KENNEL CLUB

Rare breeds in the United States have many opportunities to compete in both conformation and other events. A glance at the United Kennel Club (UKC) website (www.ukcdogs.com) tells us that the UKC is America's second-oldest and second-largest all-breed dog registry, attracting around 250,000 registrations each year. The Caucasian Mountain Dog has been registered with the UKC since 1995.

Chauncey Z. Bennett founded the UKC in 1898 with an aim to support the "total dog," meaning a dog that possesses quality in physical conformation and performance alike. With that in mind, the UKC sponsors competitive events that emphasize this "total dog" aspect. Along with traditional conformation shows, the UKC's performance events encompass just about every skill that one could imagine in a dog! These performance events include obedience, agility, coonhound trials, water races, hunting tests designed for specific types of dog (retrievers, Beagles, curs and feists, etc.) and much more. The website goes on to say, "Essentially, the UKC world of dogs is a working world. That's the way founder Chauncey Bennett designed it, and that's the way it remains today."

A bitch from Russia was awarded Best Bitch at a show in Latvia.

What many think of as traditional "dog shows" are more formally known as conformation shows. These are competitive events in which dogs are evaluated based on their conformation to their breed's standard, which is the official written description of the ideal representative of that breed. The standards recognized by the UKC are either adopted from those of Europe's canine registry, the Fédération Cynologique Internationale (FCI), or submitted by the American breed club and then revised and adopted by the UKC. At many shows, handlers will receive verbal "critiques" of their dogs; these critiques may always be

requested if not given automatically. This critique details a dog's comparison to the breed standard, and the judge also will explain why he placed each dog as he did.

UKC dog shows may be held for one breed only, several breeds or all breeds. UKC shows are arranged differently from the conformation shows of other organizations. Entries are restricted by age, and you cannot show your dog in a class other than his correct age class. When you compete for championship points, you may enter Puppy (6–12 months), Junior (1–2 years), Senior (2–3 years) or Adult (3 years and older). You may also enter the Breeder/Handler Class, where dogs of all ages compete, but the dog must be handled by his breeder or a member of the breeder's immediate family. The winners of each class compete for Best Male or Best Female. These two dogs then compete for Best of Winners; the dog who is given this award will go on to compete for Best of Breed. Best of Breed competition includes the Best of Winners and dogs that have earned Champion and Grand Champion titles. Earning Best Male or Best Female, as long as there is competition, is considered a "major."

Once a dog has earned three "majors" and accumulated 100 points, he is considered a UKC champion. What this means is that the dog is now ready to

EXPRESS YOURSELF
The most intangible of all canine attributes, expression speaks to the character of the breed, attained by the combined features of the head. The shape and balance of the dog's skull, the color and position of the eyes and the size and carriage of the head mingle to produce the correct expression of the breed. A judge may approach a dog and determine instantly whether the dog's face portrays the desired impression for the breed, conveying nobility, intelligence and alertness among other specifics of the breed standard.

compete for the title of Grand Champion, which is equivalent to an AKC championship. To earn the Grand Champion title, a dog must compete with a minimum of two other dogs who are also champions. The dog must win this class, called the Champion of Champions class, five times under three different judges. In rare breeds, it is difficult to assemble a class of champions, so the UKC Grand Champion title is truly a prestigious one. Once a dog has earned the Grand Champion title, he can continue to compete for Top Ten, but there are no further titles to earn. "Top Ten" refers to the ten dogs in each breed that have won the most points in a given year. These dogs compete in a Top Ten invitational competition annually.

dogs they own themselves. UKC shows create an atmosphere that is owner-friendly, relaxed and genuinely fun. Bait in the ring is allowed at the discretion of the judge, but throwing the bait, dropping it on the floor or other "handler tricks" will get an owner excused from the ring in a big hurry.

In addition to dog shows, the UKC offers many, many more venues for dogs and their owners, in keeping with its mission of promoting the "total dog." UKC obedience events test the training of dogs as they perform a series of prescribed exercises at the commands of their handlers. There are several levels of competition,

Although the Russian and FCI breed standards call for cropped ears, some European countries have banned ear cropping and their dogs are shown with natural ears, like the dog pictured here.

The breeds recognized by the UKC are divided into groups. The Caucasian Mountain Dog competes in the Guardian Group, which consists of dogs of similar utility and/or heritage. Depending on the show-giving club, group competition may or may not be offered. A group must have a minimum of five breeds entered in order for group competition to take place. If group competition is offered, Best in Show consists of the group winners. If there is no group competition, then all Best of Breed dogs go into the ring at the same time to compete for Best in Show. This can be a large number of dogs and thus can be very interesting, to say the least!

Aside from the variations already presented, UKC shows differ from other dog shows in one very significant way: no professional handlers are allowed to show dogs, except for those

DRESS THE PART

It's a dog show, but don't forget *your* costume. Even though the show is about the dog, you also must play your role well. You have been cast as the "dog handler" and you must smartly dress the part. Solid colors make a nice complement to the dog's coat, but choose colors that contrast. You don't want to be wearing a solid color that blends mostly or entirely with the major or only color of your dog. Whether the show is indoors or out, you still must dress properly. You want the judge to perceive you as being professional, so polish, polish, polish! And don't forget to wear sensible shoes; remember, you have to gait around the ring with your dog.

ranging from basic commands such as "sit," "come" and "heel," to advanced exercises like scent discrimination and directed retrieves over jumps, based on the dog's level of accomplishment. The classes are further delineated by the experience of the handler.

UKC obedience differs from AKC obedience in many respects. Even at the most basic levels, the dogs are expected to "honor" other dogs who are working. In other words, the "honoring" dog must be placed in a down/stay while his owner leaves the ring and moves out of sight. The dog must remain in the down/stay position while the working dog goes through the heeling exercises.

Agility events are fast-paced exercises in which the handler directs his dog through a course involving tunnels, sway bridges, jumps and other obstacles in a race against the clock. The dogs are scored according to the manner in which they negotiate the obstacles and the time elapsed to complete the course. UKC agility is very similar to AKC agility; clubs often will offer both AKC and UKC agility events (not on the same day).

Weight-pull events give certain dogs the opportunity to perform a function that comes naturally to them, and one that they obviously enjoy. Of course, not all dogs are talented or willing weight-pullers, but many are.

Basically, a dog is placed in a harness that is attached to a weighted vehicle, which the dog pulls a prescribed distance. The weighted vehicles operate either on wheels, on snow or on a rail system. The dogs are scored on how much weight they can pull; these scores are based on the proportion of the dog's body weight to the amount of weight pulled. Weight pulling requires quite a bit of training, although even the smallest breeds are allowed to participate. The most important equipment required for weight pulling is a properly fitting

SO MUCH TO DO
The bottom line is this: there is so much to do with your dog that it can be hard to decide which event to try! Just as we have to choose what to do with our weekends, so do the dogs. Whatever you choose to do with your dog, it will take training, dedication and a willingness to work with your dog to achieve a common goal, a partnership between you and your dog. There is nothing more pleasing than to watch a handler and dog performing at a high level, whether in the show ring or a competitive trial. There is something for everyone and every dog in the world of dog "showing." Dog showing should really be called "competing with your dog." You are not restricted to the traditional "dog show" and may find that your "show dog" excels in other areas as well or instead.

harness. Once the handler has dropped the harness or traces, the dog is on his own. The handler can neither bait nor call the dog, and cannot touch the dog until he has crossed the finish line and the judge has signaled a "pull."

OTHER RARE-BREED ORGANIZATIONS
In addition to the United Kennel Club, there are several other organizations that offer registration and competitive events. The availability of these events depends on geography. The IABCA (International All-Breed Canine Association of America) holds conformation shows under FCI rules. This club offers both American and international judges at all of their shows. Most of their events are held in the western US, but now also are offered in both the Midwest and Florida.

As with UKC shows, IABCA shows divide dogs by age. Dogs

Caucasian Mountain Dogs must be well-socialized to enter shows, as the show grounds are bustling with plenty of people and dogs.

are considered "puppies" up to 18 months of age for large breeds and up to 15 months of age for smaller breeds. You cannot enter your dog in any class except the appropriate class for his age. After puppyhood, you can enter your dog in the adult class. Once your dog has earned his championship, he goes on to compete for various ranks of champion, of which there are too many to enumerate here. There are fun classes as well, one of which is "Best Rare Breed in Show." This class is only offered on the Sunday of a show weekend, and only those dogs earning the highest award possible in their classes may enter (Best Puppy, Best of Breed).

In order for a dog to earn a championship, he must receive three V-1 ratings. Each dog is given a written critique during the class. The judge will ask the handler to stand near the judges' table and will either make notes or dictate to the ring steward as he compares your dog to the standard. A handler can listen while the judge does this and often the judge will ask questions, especially of handlers showing rare-breed dogs. It is a very interesting and educational procedure, to say the least. Rare breeds can earn a championship without competing against other dogs, because the dog is always competing against the breed standard. There are times when no dog in a breed receives a V-1 if none is of sufficient quality to warrant such a rating.

Another organization, the American Rare Breed Association (ARBA) holds shows across the country, although not in great numbers. In ARBA competition, as in IABCA competition, a dog can win points and earn his championship by showing against the standard, not necessarily against other dogs. The Cherry Blossom show, held annually in Washington, DC each spring, draws a handsome entry.

A show-giving group called Rarities Inc. also has arrived on the scene in the United States and Canada. This group is dedicated to the support of ancient and rare breeds. To obtain a championship, a dog requires 15 points. Of these 15 points, the dog must have attained two "majors" of at least three points under two different judges; further, the total of 15 points must have been obtained under 3 different judges. Shows with double points awarded count toward both the American and Canadian championship. To earn the International Championship, the dog must win both the American and Canadian championships. The Grand Champion title is earned by defeating 15 other Rarities or FCI champions. Grand Champions (not pending Grand Champions) may compete for the title Supreme Grand Champion,

which is earned by defeating 15 other Rarities Grand Champions. In Rarities shows, as in UKC shows, a dog must defeat other dogs in order to earn a championship. One of the unique things about Rarities Inc. is that all Working Group breeds must also pass a temperament test.

CANINE GOOD CITIZEN® PROGRAM

Have you ever considered getting your dog "certified"? The AKC's Canine Good Citizen® Program affords your dog just that opportunity. Your dog shows that he is a well-behaved canine citizen, using the basic training and good manners you have taught him, by taking a series of ten tests that illustrate that he can behave properly at home, in a public place and around other dogs. The tests are administered by participating dog clubs, colleges, 4-H clubs, Scouts and other community groups and are open to all pure-bred and mixed-breed dogs. Upon passing the ten tests, the suffix CGC is then applied to your dog's name.

The ten tests are: 1. Accepting a friendly stranger; 2. Sitting politely for petting; 3. Appearance and grooming; 4. Walking on a lead; 5. Walking through a group of people; 6. Sit, down and stay on command; 7. Coming when called; 8. Meeting another dog; 9. Calm reaction to distractions; 10. Separation from owner.

CAUCASIAN MOUNTAIN DOG

UNDERSTANDING THE CANINE MINDSET

For starters, you and your dog are on different wavelengths. Your dog is similar to a toddler in that both live in the present tense only. A dog's view of life is based primarily on cause and effect, which is similar to the old saying, "Nothing teaches a youngster to hang on like falling off the swing." If your dog stumbles down a flight of three steps, the next time he will either be more careful or avoid the steps altogether!

Your dog makes connections based on the fact that he lives in the present, so when he is doing something and you interrupt to dispense praise or a correction, a connection, positive or negative, is made. To the dog, that's like one plus one equals two! In the same sense, it's also easy to see that when your timing is off, you will cause an incorrect connection. The one-plus-one way of thinking is why you must never scold a dog for behavior that took place an hour, 15 minutes or even 5 seconds ago. But it is also why,

when your timing is perfect, you can teach him to do all kinds of wonderful things—as soon as he has made that essential connection. What helps the process is his desire to please you and to have your approval.

There are behaviors we admire in dogs, such as trustworthiness and obedience, as well as those behaviors that cause problems to a varying degree. The dog owner who encounters minor behavioral problems is wise to solve them promptly or get professional help. Bad behaviors are not corrected by repeatedly shouting "No" or getting angry with the dog. Only the giving of praise and approval for good behavior lets your dog understand right from wrong. The longer a bad behavior is allowed to continue, the harder it is to overcome. A responsible breeder is often able to help. Each dog is unique, so try not to compare your dog's behavior with your neighbor's dog or the one you had as a child.

Have your veterinarian check the dog to see whether a behavior problem could have a physical cause. An earache or toothache, for example, could be the reason for a dog to snap at you if you were to touch his head when putting on his leash. A sharp correction from you would only increase the behavior. When a physical basis is eliminated, and if the problem is not something you understand or can cope with, ask for the name of a behavioral specialist, preferably one who is familiar with the Caucasian Mountain Dog. Be sure to keep the breeder informed of your progress.

Many things, such as environment and inherited traits, form the basic behavior of a dog, just as in humans. You also must factor into his temperament the purpose for which your dog was originally bred. The major obstacle lies in the dog's inability to explain his behavior to us in a way that we understand. The one thing you should not do is to give up and abandon your dog. Somewhere a misunderstanding has occurred but, with help and patient understanding on your part, you should be able to work out the majority of bothersome behaviors.

AGGRESSION

This is a problem that concerns all responsible dog owners, and owners of the fearless Caucasian Mountain Dog must be aware of the possible problems to which aggression can lead. Aggression, when not controlled, always becomes dangerous. An aggressive

---

PROFESSIONAL HELP
Every trainer and behaviorist asks, "Why didn't you come to me sooner?" Pet owners often don't want to admit that anything is wrong with their dogs. A dog's problem often is due to the dog and his owner mixing their messages, which will only get worse. Don't put it off; consult a professional to find out whether or not the problem is serious enough to require intervention.

---

dog may lunge at, bite or even attack a person or another dog. There are different forms of dog aggression, but all are degrees of dominance, indicating that the dog, not his master, is (or thinks he is) in control. When the dog feels that he (or his control of the situation) is threatened, he will respond. The extent of the aggressive behavior varies with individual dogs. It is not at all pleasant to see bared teeth or to hear your dog growl or snarl, but these are signs of behavior that, if left uncorrected, can become extremely dangerous. A word of warning here: never challenge an aggressive dog. He is unpredictable and therefore unreliable to approach.

Nothing gets a "hello" from strangers on the street quicker than walking a puppy, but people should ask permission before petting your dog so you can tell him to sit in order to receive the admiring pats. If a hand comes down over the dog's head and he shrinks back, ask the person to bring his hand up, underneath the pup's chin. Now you're correcting strangers, too! But if you don't, it could make your dog afraid of strangers, which in turn can lead to fear biting. Socialization prevents much aggression before it rears its ugly head.

The body language of an aggressive dog about to attack is clear. The dog will have a hard, steady stare. He will try to look as big as possible by standing stiff-legged, pushing out his chest, keeping his ears up and holding his tail up and steady. The hackles on his back will rise so that a ridge of hairs stands up. This posture may include the curled lip, snarl and/or growl, or he may be silent. He looks, and definitely is, very dangerous.

By establishing rules and consistently training your Caucasian, you will be the one to emerge as pack leader.

This dominant posture is seen in dogs that are territorially aggressive. Deliverymen are constant victims of serious bites from such dogs. Territorial aggression is the reason you should never, ever, try to train a puppy to be a watchdog. It can escalate into this type of behavior over which you will have no control. All forms of aggression must be taken seriously and dealt with immediately. If signs of aggressive behavior continue, or grow worse, or if you are at all unsure about how to deal with your dog's behavior, get the help of a professional.

Uncontrolled aggression, sometimes called "irritable aggression," is not something for the pet owner to try to solve. If you cannot solve your dog's dangerous behavior with professional help, and you (quite rightly) do not wish to keep a canine time-bomb in your home, you will have some important decisions to make. Aggressive dogs often cannot be rehomed successfully, as they are dangerous and unreliable in their behavior. An aggressive dog should be dealt with only by someone who knows exactly the situation that he is getting into and has the experience, dedication and ideal living environment to attempt rehabilitating the dog, which may not be possible. In these cases, the dog ends up having to be humanely put down. Making a decision about euthanasia is not an easy

undertaking for anyone, for any reason, but you cannot pass on to another home a dog that you know could cause harm.

A milder form of aggression is the dog's guarding anything that he perceives to be his—his food dish, his toys, his bed and/or his crate. This can be prevented if you take firm control from the start. The young puppy can and should be taught that his leader will share, but that certain rules apply. Guarding is mild aggression only in the beginning stages, and it will worsen and become dangerous if you let it.

Don't try to snatch anything away from your puppy. Bargain for the item in question so that you can positively reinforce him when he gives it up. Punishment only results in worsening any aggressive behavior.

Many dogs extend their guarding impulse toward items they've stolen. The dog figures, "If I have it, it's mine!" (Some ill-behaved kids have similar tendencies.) An angry confrontation will only increase the dog's aggression. (Have you ever watched a child have a tantrum?) Try a simple distraction first, such as tossing a toy or picking up his leash for a walk. If that doesn't work, the best way to handle the situation is with basic obedience. Show the dog a treat, followed by calm, almost slow-motion commands: "Come. Sit. Drop it. Good dog,"

INTER-CANINE AGGRESSION

Males are usually the ones given the "dog-aggressive" label, but both males and females can be aggressive toward dogs of their own sex, which is why good breeders will sometimes persuade the owner of a female to add a male puppy, not another female. Early spaying or neutering helps but is not guaranteed to squelch all aggressive behavior.

Aggression is a dominant behavior, which is why you have repeatedly been told to socialize your puppy with other dogs as well as with people outside the family. Dogs that have not had the benefit of socialization experiences are ripe for becoming dog-aggressive.

If you pull back on the leash as your dog meets another, you are signaling to your dog that you are afraid. The message goes right down the leash. His aggressive attitude in that case is your dog's way of protecting you. If you correct him for it, you'll have one very confused dog! If you are confronted with a dog that you consider or know to be aggressive, the best solution is to turn your dog's head away from the other dog (a head collar makes it easy to do) in order to break eye contact between the two. Then cross the street if you have to, crouch down to your dog's level and call him to you so you can praise him for a "good come."

If your dog gets into a true dogfight, stay out of it. Drop your dog's leash. Any intervention on your part will only exacerbate the aggression of both dogs, and you are sure to be bitten.

Mom knows best and is the pups' very first teacher, educating them in the ways of being part of a pack.

from a strange dog and when to stop overly exciting play with their own puppy.

Fear biting is yet another aggressive behavior. A fear biter gives many warning signals. The dog leans away from the approaching person (sometimes hiding behind his owner) with his ears and tail down, but not in submission. He may even shiver. His hackles are raised, his lips curled. When the person steps into the dog's "flight zone" (a circle of 1 to 3 feet surrounding the dog), he attacks. Because of the fear factor, he performs a rapid attack-and-retreat. Because it is directed at a person, vets are often the victims of this form of aggression. It is frightening, but discovering and eliminating the cause of the fright will help overcome the dog's need to bite. Early socialization again plays a strong role in the prevention of this behavior. Again, if you can't cope with it, get the help of an expert.

and then hand over the cheese! That's one example of positive-reinforcement training.

Children can be bitten when they try to retrieve a stolen shoe or toy, so they need to know how to handle the dog or to let an adult do it. They may also be bitten as they run away from a dog, in either fear or play. The dog sees the child's running as reason for pursuit, and even a friendly young puppy will nip at the heels of a runaway. Teach the kids not to run away

DOMINANCE
Dogs are born with dominance skills, meaning that they can be quite clever in trying to get their way. The "follow-me" trot to the cookie jar is an example. The toy dropped in your lap says "Play with me." The leash delivered to you along with an excited look means "Take me for a walk." These are all good-natured dominant behaviors. Ask your dog to sit before agreeing to his request and you'll remain "top dog."

CHEWING
All puppies chew. All dogs chew. This is a fact of life for canines, and sometimes you may think it's what your dog does best! A pup starts chewing when his first set of teeth erupts and continues throughout the teething period. Chewing gives the pup relief from itchy gums and incoming teeth and, from that time on, he gets great satisfaction out of this

normal, somewhat idle, canine activity. Providing safe chew toys is the best way to direct this behavior in an appropriate manner. Chew toys are available in all sizes, textures and flavors, but you must monitor the wear-and-tear inflicted on your pup's toys to be sure that the ones you've chosen are safe and remain in good condition.

Puppies cannot distinguish between a rawhide toy and a nice leather shoe or wallet. It's up to you to keep your possessions away from the dog and to keep your eye on the dog. There's a form of destruction caused by chewing that is not the dog's fault. Let's say you allow him on the sofa. One day he takes a rawhide bone up on the sofa and, in the course of chewing on the bone, takes up a bit of fabric. He continues to chew. Disaster! Now you've learned the lesson: dogs with chew toys have to be either kept off furniture and carpets, carefully supervised or put into their confined areas for chew time.

The wooden legs of furniture are favorite objects for chewing. The first time, tell the dog "Leave it!" (or "No!") and offer him a chew toy as a substitute. But your clever dog may be hiding under the chair and doing some silent destruction, which you may not notice until it's too late. In this case, it's time to try one of the foul-tasting products, made specifically

I CAN'T SMILE WITHOUT YOU

How can you tell whether your dog is suffering from separation anxiety? Not every dog who enjoys a close bond with his owner will suffer from separation anxiety. In actuality, only a small percentage of dogs are affected. Separation anxiety manifests itself in dogs older than one year of age and may not occur until the dog is a senior. A number of destructive behaviors are associated with the problem, including scratch marks in front of doorways, bite marks on furniture, drool stains on furniture and flooring and tattered draperies, carpets or cushions. The most reliable sign of separation anxiety is howling and crying when the owner leaves and then barking like mad for extended periods. Affected dogs may also defecate or urinate throughout the home, attempt to escape when the door opens, vocalize excessively and show signs of depression (including loss of appetite, listlessness and lack of activity).

to prevent destructive chewing, that is sprayed on the objects of your dog's chewing attention. These products also work to keep the dog away from plants, trash, etc. It's even a good way to stop the dog from "mouthing" or chewing on your hands or the leg of your pants. (Be sure to wash your hands after the mouthing lesson!) A little spray goes a long way.

THE MACHO DOG

The Venus/Mars differences are found in dogs, too. Males have distinct behaviors that, while seemingly sex-related, are more closely connected to the role of the male as leader. Marking territory by urinating on it is one means that male dogs use to establish their presence. Doing so merely says, "I've been here." Small dogs often attempt to lift their legs higher on the tree than the previous male. While this is natural behavior outdoors on items like telephone poles, fence posts, fire hydrants and most other upright objects, marking indoors is totally unacceptable. Treat it as you would a house-training accident and clean thoroughly to eradicate the scent.

Another behavior often seen in the macho male, mounting is a dominance display. Neutering the dog before six months of age helps to deter this behavior. You can discourage him from mounting by catching the dog as he's about to mount you, stepping quickly aside and saying "Off!"

DIGGING

Digging is another natural and normal doggy behavior. Wild canines dig to bury whatever food they can save for later to eat. (And you thought *we* invented the doggy bag!) Burying bones or toys is a primary cause to dig. Dogs also dig to get at interesting little underground creatures like moles and mice. Caucasians, being primitive in many ways, dig holes to

sleep in, to stay cool from the sun and to stay warm in the winter. The solution to the last two is easy. In the summer, provide a bed that's up off the ground and placed in a shaded area. In winter, the dog should be indoors to sleep, either in the house or in an adequate insulated kennel. To understand how natural and normal this is, you have only to consider the Nordic breeds of sled dog who, at the end of the run, routinely dig a bed for themselves in the snow. It's the nesting instinct. How often have you seen your dog go round and round in circles, pawing at his blanket or bedding before flopping down to sleep?

Domesticated dogs also dig to escape, and that's a lot more dangerous than it is destructive. A dog that digs under the fence is the one that is hit by a car or becomes lost. A good fence to protect a digger should be set 12 inches below ground level, and every fence needs to be routinely checked for even the smallest openings that can become possible escape routes.

Catching your dog in the act of digging is the easiest way to stop it, because your dog will make the "one-plus-one" connection, but digging is too often a solitary occupation, something the lonely dog does out of boredom. Catch your young puppy in the act and put a stop to it before you have a yard full of craters. It is more difficult to stop if your dog sees you gardening. If you can dig, why can't he? Because you say so, that's why! Some dogs are excavation experts, and some dogs never dig. However, when it comes to any of these instinctive canine behaviors, never say "never."

JUMPING UP

Jumping up is a device of enthusiastic, attention-seeking puppies, but adult dogs often like to jump up as well, usually as a form of canine greeting. This is a controversial issue. Some owners wouldn't have it any other way! They encourage their dogs, and the owners and dogs alike enjoy the friendly physical contact. Some owners think that it's cute when it comes from a puppy, but not from an adult. Conversely, there are those who consider jumping up to be one of the worst kinds of bad manners to be found in a dog. Among this group inevitably are bound to be some of your best friends. Regardless, the Caucasian is a large dog and his jumping up can be intimidating to anyone.

There are two situations in which your dog should be restrained from any and all jumping up. One is around children, especially young children and those who are not at ease with dogs. The other is when you are entertaining guests. No one who comes dressed up for a party

Just another day—digging, marking—the usual dog stuff!

wants to be groped by your dog, no matter how friendly his intentions or how clean his paws.

Hopefully, you took our earlier advice about discouraging jumping in the puppy. If you have a jumpy adult, though, the answer is relatively simple. If the dog has already started to jump up, the first command is "Off," followed immediately by "Sit." The dog must sit every time you are about to meet a friend on the street or when someone enters your home, be it child or adult. You may have to ask people to ignore the dog for a few minutes in order to let his urge for an enthusiastic greeting subside. If your dog is too exuberant and won't sit still, you'll have to work harder by first telling him "Off" and then issuing the down-stay command. This requires more work on your part, because the down is a submissive position and your dog is only trying to be super-friendly. A small treat is expected when training for this particular down.

If you have a real pet peeve about a dog's jumping up, then disallow it from the day your puppy comes home. Jumping up is a subliminally taught human-to-dog greeting. Dogs don't greet each other in this way. It begins because your puppy is close to the ground and he's easier to pet and cuddle if he reaches up and you bend over to meet him halfway. If you won't like it later, don't start it when he is young, but do give lots of praise and affection for a good sit.

BARKING
Your Caucasian Mountain Dog has been blessed with a booming Russian voice and the will to use it. His protective instincts, coupled with his suspicious nature, give him lots of opportunity to bark. This, of course, varies from dog to dog, so some Caucasian Mountain Dogs may talk more than others. It's vital to train the puppy to keep quiet from an early age, unless there's a reason for his chatter.

Talkative dogs can be somewhat frustrating to us owners, as it is not always easy to tell what a dog means by his bark—is he excited, happy, frightened or angry? Whatever it is that the dog is trying to say, he should not be punished for barking. It is only when the barking becomes excessive, and when the excessive barking becomes a bad habit, that the behavior needs to be modi-

fied. Remember, too, that the Caucasian Mountain Dog is a nocturnal barker, a trait that will not make you very popular in your neighborhood.

The Caucasian Mountain Dog on duty, when sensibly trained, will use his voice purposefully to sound a serious warning. If an intruder came into your home in the middle of the night and your Caucasian Mountain Dog barked an alarm, wouldn't you be pleased? You would probably deem your dog a hero, a wonderful guardian and protector of the home. On the other hand, if a friend drops by unexpectedly, rings the doorbell and is greeted with a sudden sharp bark, you would probably be annoyed at the dog. But in reality, isn't this just the same behavior? The dog does not know any better. Unless he sees who is at the door and it is someone he knows, he will bark as a means of vocalizing that his (and your) territory is being threatened. While your friend is not posing a threat, it is all the same to the dog. Barking is his means of letting you know that there is an intrusion, whether friend or foe, on your property. This type of barking is instinctive and should not be discouraged.

Excessive habitual barking, however, is a problem that should be corrected early on, and Caucasians can become nuisance barkers if not properly trained from a young age. As your Caucasian Mountain Dog grows up, you will be able to tell when his barking is

The Caucasian Mountain Dog and livestock are part of each other's heritage.

JUST SAY NO!

You love your dog and want to let him know it! You might think, then, how better to show him than by tossing him a treat from the table? After all, he is part of the family, right? All dogs respond to food and know that it signals good things. Plus, many dogs are quite crafty when it comes to pleading for a bite of something tasty—and many owners are quite weak when it comes to resisting their dogs' imploring eyes and adorable beseeching faces.

Be strong: resist and just say no! Apart from the instant gratification that the dog receives, there is nothing beneficial about feeding your dog from the table. You've already done your research to find a complete diet, so why unbalance it? Plus, an excited beggar eating table scraps runs the risk of bloat.

There are better ways to show your dog that you care and to reinforce your bond. In the second it takes to "throw him a bone," figuratively speaking, you can give him a friendly pat. Or you may choose from the start not to allow your dog into the room when the family is eating. Feed him in another room while the family is having its meal, thus establishing his daily feeding schedule. Remember, it's much more difficult to break a dog's begging habit than it is to never allow him to beg in the first place.

purposeful and when it is for no reason. You will become able to distinguish your dog's different barks and their meanings. It is similar to a person's tone of voice, except that the dog has to rely totally on tone of voice because he does not have the benefit of using words. An incessant barker will be evident at an early age.

There are some things that encourage a dog to bark. For example, if your dog barks non-stop for a few minutes and you give him a treat to quiet him, he believes that you are rewarding him for barking. He will associate barking with getting a treat and will keep doing it until he is rewarded. On the other hand, if you give him a command such as "Quiet" and praise him after he has stopped barking for a few seconds, he will get the idea that being "quiet" is what you want him to do.

INDEX

My Caucasian Mountain Dog

PUT YOUR PUPPY'S FIRST PICTURE HERE

Dog's Name _____

Date _____ Photographer _____